HERB

Published by Inkshares Inc., San Francisco, California
www.inkshares.com

Edited and designed by Girl Friday Productions
www.girlfridayproductions.com

Cover design by Todd Bates

ISBN: 9781941758250
eISBN: 9781941758274
Library of Congress Control Number: 2015938851

First edition

Printed in China

HERB

Mastering the Art of Cooking with Cannabis

Chefs **Laurie Wolf** & **Melissa Parks**
with the team at **HERB**

Photography by **Bruce Wolf**

Dear Reader,

We are immensely proud of this book. It integrates technique in an accessible manner and balances exotic recipes with more homey, comfortable kitchen mainstays. More than anything, we are proud to treat cannabis as exactly what it is: just another herb (albeit a unique and amazing one).

But prior to your embarking on what we hope to be a flavorful and relaxing journey, we wanted to speak to the realities of culinary cannabis and ensure that you set sail responsibly.

First, cannabis is still illegal in many countries and is still illegal at the federal level here in the United States. While many states and municipalities have legalized cannabis consumption, this book is in no way an encouragement to break applicable laws. It is our expectation that these recipes will be enjoyed within the borders of ongoing state-level deregulation or applicable foreign legal regimes. Importantly, even where medicinal or recreational cannabis is legal (at the writing of this, twenty-three states and the District of Columbia have legalized cannabis in either medicinal or recreational form), there are still significant and wise prohibitions on what one may do under the influence of cannabis (just as while under the influence of alcohol). A good place to start would be with a simple Googling of the applicable cannabis laws in the jurisdiction in which you are enjoying these pages.

Second, the information contained within these pages isn't medical (or legal) advice: *Herb*'s counsel is only of the culinary form. While it discusses molecules and medicinal applications, this is only a summarization, rather than an endorsement, of existing opinions and facts. If you are intending to use cannabis for medical purposes, you should first consult with a physician. And if you have never consumed cannabis before, regardless of any recreational intent, you should consult with a physician to ensure that you are healthy enough to enjoy cannabis responsibly (sorry, we know we sound like a Cialis ad). Nothing in this book is a substitute for consultation with a physician.

Third, spend time getting to know your budtender and understand the levels of psychoactive compounds such as THC in your cannabis. Just as one ounce of 100 proof gin will get you more inebriated than one ounce of 70 proof gin, buds with higher THC or CBD levels will have a far more potent effect despite having the same weight. The recipes and dosing methodologies outlined in this book assume levels of 12 percent; higher or lower levels in the cannabis you use will result in a stronger or weaker high (all of this is discussed in the early parts of this text, which should be read prior to attempting any of the recipes). One of the most positive effects of legalization is to create a regulatory environment that, much like with alcohol, provides us with more knowledge of the probable effects of what we are ingesting. Some of the most important parts of this book take place outside the kitchen—in getting to know your budtender and understanding exactly what you are purchasing (or growing).

Fourth, while this book presents a large number and wide array of recipes, it is not meant to encourage overly frequent consumption of cannabis. While a physician may prescribe frequent consumption for medical purposes, this book does not endorse enjoying these recipes as anything other than occasional complements to non-medicated foods. Similarly, when crafting meals, rather than preparing multiple infused courses, choose one course and see how that affects you and your consenting guests. To quote one of our favorite lines by a known cannabis enthusiast, take "baby steps." Begin slowly. Use oils and butters of less strength, gradually getting used to how cannabis affects you—there are many recipes in this book, and you can always try them again.

Finally, in the simplest terms possible, use good judgment. We suggest that you label all cannabis products so that people don't inadvertently ingest them. That means labeling both cannabutters and cannaoils, and also any leftovers. Given the delayed nature of the high with most edibles, one could unknowingly ingest cannabis only to have the effects hit them at a later time (for instance, while driving a car). Don't feed cannabis-infused products to guests without their consent or knowledge. Don't feed it to someone who is pregnant or ingest it if you are pregnant yourself. Under no circumstances should one provide medicated foods to a child unless by order of a physician. Nobody under the age of eighteen should undertake the recipes in this book or ingest the edibles surveyed in this book. Even just enjoying cannabis yourself, as an adult, don't do strange activities or things you have not done before.

The words on these pages are not a comprehensive list of sound cautions or sensible prohibitions. Cannabis may just be an "herb," but it is an herb with unique effects. To borrow some apt words often employed in the context of alcohol: enjoy responsibly.

Very truly yours,

Inkshares

CONTENTS

SANDWICHES

PIZZA, PASTAS, AND RISOTTO

ENTRÉES

DRINKS

BAKED GOODS

COOKIES AND DESSERTS

INTRODUCTION

Welcome to *Herb: Mastering the Art of Cooking with Cannabis.* Within these pages, we hope you find the inspiration and knowledge you need to take your cannabis cooking skills to a new level. Whether you're a home cook or a professional chef, you'll find well-researched information, cutting-edge techniques, and beautiful recipes to delight and inspire.

Cooking with cannabis began as a clandestine hobby, a way for those who wouldn't (or couldn't) smoke it to achieve the desired effect. Yet incorporating cannabis into food has fast become an art form, with more-sophisticated dishes and better understanding that both accommodates and transforms the herb's unique flavor. Looking forward, we hope that cooking with cannabis will be treated with the same level of respect and enthusiasm afforded to more-traditional culinary techniques.

Though the common perception is that people use cannabis to get high, for many people, consuming cannabis is not simply about attaining an altered mental state. Sufferers of epilepsy and seizures, patients with chronic and agonizing pain, people seeking relief from stress and anxiety—these individuals and others all benefit from the effects of cannabis and THC.

As cannabis legalization spreads, the humble medicinal plant is being brought out of the darkness and increasingly viewed as the beneficial and positive herb that it is. As more people experiment with ways to work with cannabis, and puzzle over terpenes and CBD and dosing levels, the need for solid authoritative information and well-tested recipes grows as well.

OUR HOPE FOR *HERB*

Our goal in the pages ahead is to help educate you about cannabis and the incredible variety of ways it can be used and consumed. We want to dispel the myths you may have heard, and encourage you to explore cooking with this wonderful ingredient. By framing cannabis as we and many others see it—as a beneficial herb with pleasant effects—

we hope you'll consider that a cannabis cookbook is no more outlandish or outside the mainstream than a book on cocktails might be. Through the delicious recipes that follow, we invite you to experience and enjoy cannabis's effects and benefits in the privacy of your own home. Perhaps you'll even be inspired to create culinary masterpieces of your own!

A NOTE ON DOSING

In areas where cannabis is difficult or illegal to obtain, users have struggled with determining the strength of the particular strain or the effects that various methods of ingestion could have—this could mean they feel little to no effect from a given dish, or, on the other hand, have an unpleasantly strong experience. Fortunately, burgeoning cannabis legalization and the growth of official dispensaries mean that consumers can be much more informed about the product they are purchasing. Even still, it's often difficult to gauge the effects of a particular strain in advance.

In this book, we've attempted to make cooking with cannabis a more reliable and replicable endeavor. We've done meticulous research on the effects of cannabis in various recipes and have developed a proper set of guidelines to assist you in choosing the correct dosage for your meal. See "Dosing" on page 26 for more specifics.

SKILLS AND EQUIPMENT

We wrote this book for a wide range of folks. You might be cooking for a dinner party, preparing a dish or a meal for someone who uses cannabis medicinally, or simply whipping up a quick snack for yourself. With that in mind, we've labeled each recipe with a degree of difficulty, so whether you're a chef or a beginner who has trouble sautéing a vegetable, there will be something in this book for you.

Similarly, we wanted the cooking process to be a simple, intuitive one. To that end, you won't need anything beyond the culinary equipment found in an ordinary kitchen. To introduce cannabis into the dishes that follow, you will prepare an extraction by infusing cannabis into a medium such as oil or butter, and then use the extraction as directed in the recipe. The recipes for the extractions begin on page 28.

THE FINE PRINT

Cannabis is a controversial substance. It is banned for recreational use in many places and entirely illegal in others. *Herb: Mastering the Art of Cooking with Cannabis* is intended for those who have legal and legitimate access to cannabis and are of legal age to prepare edibles. If you're cooking from this book, we expect that you have purchased your cannabis from a reputable dispensary and therefore have an idea of the strain and strength you're working with. We strongly encourage the responsible and legal use of this herb and believe that by demonstrating its safety and beneficial properties, we can help the legalization movement.

As legalization of cannabis spreads, more research into its beneficial medicinal effects is being conducted. Where possible, we have included links and references to medical research to provide you with accurate and scientifically endorsed information.

CANNABIS 101

When you cook with cannabis, you're working with an herb that has a long history and many interesting and beneficial properties. However, it's also plagued by an aura of misinformation. Learning about cannabis's history, properties, and benefits not only elevates your appreciation for this herb but also helps spread accurate information and moves the legalization movement forward.

WHAT CANNABIS IS

If you're cooking with a plant or an herb, it's good to know a little about where it came from and how it's been used in the past. Cannabis is no exception. As a budding cannabis chef (pun intended), you should know the basics.

Cannabis is usually derived from the *Cannabis sativa* plant, which grows naturally in many tropical and temperate areas of the world. These days, however, it's more commonly grown hydroponically (without soil) indoors. The main active ingredient in cannabis is called delta-9-tetrahydrocannabinol, more commonly known as THC. This is the part of the plant that makes you high. But the rest of the plant has been used for thousands of years.

The oldest written record of cannabis use comes from the Chinese emperor Shen Nung in 2727 BC. The ancient Greeks and Romans used cannabis in ceremonies and were aware of its psychoactive effects. It came to the Western Hemisphere in 1545 when the Spaniards imported it to Chile for use as fiber. In North America, in colonial times, cannabis, in the form of hemp, was grown on many plantations for use in rope, clothing, sails, and paper. George Washington himself cultivated hemp at Mount Vernon for use in repairing fishing nets.

HOW CANNABIS IS USED TODAY

Cannabis is now more commonly used as a recreational drug—modern growers intentionally breed strains to produce the strongest psychoactive effect. In fact, it has become one of the most widely used illicit drugs in the world. This is primarily because it's easy to prepare and obtain, easy to consume, and its effects are usually not intense or forceful, making it attractive to people from all walks of life. It generally has a relaxing, happy effect, and wears off without any significant hangover.

Cannabis is consumed in three main forms: marijuana, hashish, and hash oil. Marijuana is made from the dried flowers and leaves of the cannabis plant. It is the least potent of all the cannabis products and is usually the form that is smoked or made into edible products. Hashish is made from the resin (a secreted gum) of the cannabis plant. It is dried and pressed into small blocks and smoked. It can also be added to food and eaten. Hash oil, the most potent cannabis product, is a thick oil derived from hashish; it is also eaten or smoked.

Cannabis is most commonly smoked in hand-rolled cigarettes (known as joints) or in special water pipes (bongs). These bongs can be bought, or made from things such as juice containers, soda cans, or even apples. Bongs are designed to allow the smoke to pass through water before being inhaled, cooling the smoke and making it less harsh on the throat.

CANNABIS TERMS

Cannabis has a long history of use in many countries, and as a result, a lot of terminology has arisen around it. Here's a short list of cannabis lingo.

Cannabis: The name given to the plant variants *Cannabis sativa, Cannabis indica,* and *Cannabis ruderalis.*

Marijuana: A more general or informal term used to describe cannabis. It's believed to come from the Spanish names Maria (Mary) and Juana (Joan or Jane), which gave rise to the slang term Mary Jane.

Cannabinoids: A class of chemical compounds found in cannabis that act on cannabinoid receptors in the human brain.

THC: A cannabinoid, and the main psychoactive ingredient of cannabis. It's also known as delta–9–tetrahydrocannabinol.

CBD: Another cannabinoid, also known as cannabidiol. It doesn't get you high, but studies have shown that it has a number of medical benefits. Clinical trials are under way to test its effectiveness for treating conditions such as schizophrenia, epilepsy, and cancer.

Edible: Any food product, such as brownies, that contains THC.

Hashish: Hashish, or hash, is a cannabis product composed of compressed or purified preparations of cannabis resin. It contains the same active ingredients (such as THC) as cannabis buds or leaves, but often in higher concentrations. The word *hashish* comes from an Arabic word for grass. It is consumed by being heated in a pipe, hookah, bong, or other implement; mixed with cannabis buds or tobacco and smoked in joints; smoked as bottle tokes (also known as brewing bots or bucket bongs); or made into edibles, especially sweets.

Hash oil: Hash oil—also known as hashish oil, BHO (butane hash oil), wax, shatter, crumble, honey oil, dabs, or budder—is another form of cannabis. It is a resinous mix of cannabinoids obtained from the cannabis plant by solvent extraction, after which it is formed into a hardened or viscous mass. Hash oil is the most potent of the main cannabis products because of its high level of psychoactive compound by volume.

Hemp: The material from certain strains of *Cannabis sativa* that have been bred specifically for fiber, oils and topical ointments; edible seeds; and a wide and growing variety of other purposes that don't involve intoxication.

Terpenes: A class of organic compounds produced by some plants and insects. Terpenes contribute to the scent, flavor, and colors of different cannabis varieties.

WHERE CANNABIS IS LEGAL

The legality of cannabis for recreational use varies by country. Since the widespread prohibition of cannabis began in the late 1930s, its possession and use have been illegal in most countries. Recently, however, the possession of small quantities of cannabis has been decriminalized, largely for medicinal purposes, especially in parts of North and South America and Europe.

United States federal law prohibits using, selling, or possessing cannabis. However, state laws regarding cannabis differ from the federal laws. As of this writing, the recreational use of cannabis is legal in Colorado, Washington, Oregon, Alaska, and the District of Columbia, and more states seem to be moving in that direction. In addition, more than twenty states now have legalized medical marijuana programs.

As of this writing, Uruguay is the only country to have fully legalized the recreational use and cultivation

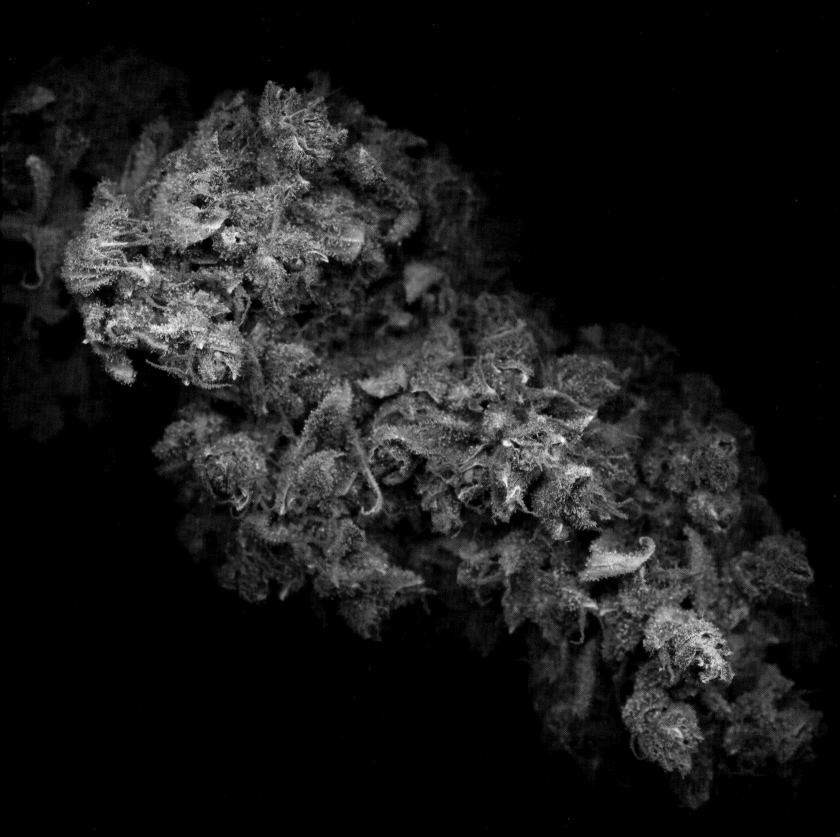

of cannabis. However, over the last three decades, global cannabis policies have begun to budge, giving us hope for an herb-friendly future.

HOW CANNABIS IS GROWN

Cannabis may be colloquially known as "weed," but don't let the slang term fool you—flower-producing marijuana doesn't just pop up anywhere. Just like producing exceptional grapes for wine or hops for beer, getting a flavorful, consumable crop out of your plants takes ample amounts of time, patience, and craft.

The majority of the marijuana that we consume comes from the flowering bud of the female cannabis plant. The flower is the most terpene- and cannabinoid-dense part of the plant, making it the portion that's typically harvested for use both medically and recreationally.

Many different growing methods and philosophies are utilized around the world, and most of them aim to get as many budding flowers as possible. Cannabis can be grown both indoors and outdoors; while outdoor growing is easier, and far more sustainable and cost effective, marijuana's illegal status in many places has led cannabis producers to develop elaborate and capital-intensive indoor growing systems to avoid prosecution and provide security for their crop.

Indoor growers often use equipment such as hydroponic systems, networks of lights that emit the optimal spectrum for growth, supplementary fertilizers or organic nutrients, and humidity-controlled chambers in an attempt to get the best yield.

Marijuana plants grown outdoors require less maintenance, and tend to grow much larger and produce heavier yields. In much of the world, however, climate limits the herb to one crop per growing season. Of course, those lucky enough to live near the equator avoid this problem entirely.

Outdoor growing takes advantage of a plant's natural food: sunlight. Not only do some claim that sun-grown marijuana is more flavorful, but growing outdoors drastically reduces the carbon footprint of cannabis production. In fact, one 2012 study calculated that the fossil fuels needed to power one commercial warehouse of indoor cannabis equated to that of 3 million cars.[1]

WHERE CANNABIS GROWS

Originally domesticated in South and Central Asia, cannabis has become the most widely grown illicit substance in the world.

Wild *Cannabis ruderalis* can be found in some parts of Central Europe. The Netherlands, Portugal, and Spain are the European countries currently thought to be the most cannabis-tolerant regions.

In the Americas, Mexico and Paraguay have been labeled the biggest suppliers of illicit cannabis. Uruguay's legalization and the wave of support the decision received among other Latin American countries may very soon turn the tables on the illicit cannabis trade throughout North and South America.

If you're fortunate enough to live in one of the US states where cannabis is legal, chances are your cannabis was grown a relatively short distance away from you.

THE EFFECTS AND MEDICAL BENEFITS OF CANNABIS

HOW CANNABIS IS CONSUMED

Cannabis can be consumed in a number of ways to produce a high. The most common method involves smoking, but it can also be inhaled via a vaporizer, or eaten.

Each method of consumption produces a different effect, based on how your body processes the active ingredients in the cannabis.

The downside to smoking cannabis is that the inhaled smoke and some of the toxins that come as a result of combustion are not good for the lungs. Also, a large proportion of the cannabinoids and THC in cannabis are lost when exhaling the smoke.

A vaporizer, which is a device that gently heats cannabis to around 365° to 410°F (185° to 210°C), causes the active ingredients in cannabis to evaporate into a gas that doesn't include the toxic by-products of burning or smoking. Modern vaporizers are small and portable and look like electronic cigarettes. They usually take capsules or liquid forms of cannabis, although some can heat the herb directly.

Ingesting cannabis orally—in food, for example—is much safer than smoking in terms of toxins. It is processed by the liver, rather than the lungs, and the results pass into the brain more quickly and easily than smoked cannabis, despite the initial delay resulting from the fact that the cannabis has been digested. The effects take longer to present themselves and last longer. When ingested, cannabis's primary active component, delta–9–tetrahydrocannabinol, is converted by the liver to the more psychoactive 11-hydroxy-delta-9-tetrahydrocannabinol and is considered to have a more powerful effect than that achieved through smoking.

This stronger and longer-lasting high can be a little scary to inexperienced users. People new to cannabis are often advised to ingest only a small amount of an edible their first time, and wait considerably longer than seems appropriate before eating more. This is to avoid the temptation to overeat under the assumption that the edibles are not working, and then become unpleasantly stoned when the effects do kick in. See "Dosing" on page 26 for more information.

Regardless of the process of consumption, it's important that the primary cannabinoid in the cannabis, tetrahydrocannabinolic acid, be turned into psychoactive THC in order to have an effect. This process is called decarboxylation, or "decarbing," and happens when cannabis is heated. During smoking or vaporizing, this heating happens automatically, but when you're eating cannabis or using it in food preparation, it is important that the cannabis is decarboxylated first, to release its full psychoactive effect. (See "Decarboxylation" on page 26 for a description of the process.)

THC and other cannabinoids are more efficiently absorbed into the bloodstream when combined with butter and other lipids or, to a lesser extent, dissolved in ethanol. The time to onset of effects depends strongly on stomach contents (i.e., consuming edibles on an empty stomach will result in a quicker high), but is commonly around one to two hours.

HOW CANNABIS AFFECTS THE MIND AND BODY

Cannabis affects many of the same areas of the brain that are targeted by heroin, cocaine, and alcohol.

Depending on the quantity, quality, and method of consumption, cannabis can produce a feeling of euphoria—the high—by stimulating brain cells to release a chemical called dopamine. When smoked or inhaled, the feeling of euphoria is almost immediate. When ingested in food, however, it can take much longer, even hours, for the drug to signal the brain to release dopamine.

The high can also bring about mood changes. Unlike alcohol or other drugs, it's very rare that these effects include violence, aggression, or hostility. This is one of the reasons pro-marijuana campaigners fight so strongly to have the drug decriminalized—they cite cannabis as an alternative to alcohol and methamphetamine-related drugs, which can produce those negative effects.

Under the influence of cannabis, users frequently report being relaxed, and some experience heightened sensory perception, with colors appearing more vivid and noises being louder. Cannabis can create an altered perception of time and lead to increased appetite, known as the "munchies." It also causes increased heart rate and dry mouth (commonly referred to as cotton-mouth), and triggers blood vessels in the eyes to expand (producing bloodshot eyes).

The impact of cannabis on an individual can vary based on many factors, including how often and how recently they have used the drug, and the drug's strength.

Cannabis does have some negative effects, according to the National Institutes of Health.[2] These may include feelings of panic, anxiety, and fear (paranoia); hallucinations; trouble concentrating; decreased ability to perform tasks that require coordination; and decreased interest in completing tasks.

In addition, when coming down from the high, users may feel depressed or extremely tired. While cannabis use generally produces a mellow experience, it can heighten agitation, anxiety, insomnia, and irritability in some people.

IS CANNABIS ADDICTIVE?

Many cannabis users worry about whether or not they will become addicted. There is a lot of debate on this issue. According to *The Science of Marijuana*, written by Leslie L. Iversen, a professor of pharmacology at the University of Oxford, somewhere between 10 percent and 30 percent of regular users will develop dependency. Only around 9 percent will suffer a serious addiction.

Also, in general, cannabis has very few severe withdrawal symptoms. These symptoms can include anxiety, depression, nausea, sleep disturbances, and gastrointestinal problems.

THE MEDICAL BENEFITS OF CANNABIS

Historically speaking, the demonization of cannabis is a relatively recent phenomenon. In fact, up until 1942, cannabis extract was regularly prescribed by doctors in the US for labor pains, rheumatism, and nausea.[3]

Studying cannabis has led to a better understanding of the chemicals that influence our behavior and how we experience them. After THC was isolated in the 1960s, researchers were able to follow its path in the body. This pointed them in the direction of a much larger and much more complex biochemical system than they had anticipated: the endocannabinoid system.[4]

The endocannabinoid system is a network of special kinds of cell receptors that are found in specific regions of the brain and throughout the body. These cell receptors respond to chemical triggers that influence everything from sleep and appetite to muscle reflexes, mood, and deep-thinking skills.[5] Cannabinoids and terpenes found in the marijuana plant are capable of binding to and interacting with the endocannabinoid system, triggering some of the plant's medicinal qualities, as well as its psychoactive ones.

In addition, cannabis's terpene-dense flower is rich in antioxidants and coated in anti-inflammatory, antifungal, and antibacterial compounds.

Research has shown that cannabis may be effective in treating the following conditions: asthma, cancer, depression, epileptic disorders, pain, post-traumatic stress disorder, and addiction to harmful substances such as methadone.

This is really just the tip of the iceberg, as cannabis has shown tremendous promise as a potential treatment for a variety of other ailments. Cannabis science is not well known to the public; however, if you hop online and do a little digging, you can learn more.

CANNABIS STRAINS

The cannabis strains generally consumed today are *Cannabis sativa* and *Cannabis indica*, or hybrids of the two, cultivated to contain a high percentage of cannabinoids. *Cannabis ruderalis* (the third cannabis strain) has a low THC content and is difficult to harvest, so it is rarely used for consumption.

Cannabis breeding has grown dramatically in the last few years because some strains are said to be worth millions. For example, a high-CBD, low-THC variety called Charlotte's Web has garnered praise for its ability to reduce seizures without making patients feel the typical, cerebral high.[6]

THE DIFFERENCE BETWEEN STRAINS

Generally speaking, indica strains have a sedative, soporific, pain-relieving, and time-slowing effect. These cannabis plants are often short, squat, and bushy. Their buds are fatter than sativa buds and produce large amounts of THC resin. Indica plants are generally easier to grow, have a heftier yield, and finish growing much faster than sativa strains. As a result, in many places it is easier to find indica than sativa.

In contrast to indica, sativa cannabis creates an uplifting, soaring, spacey, giggly, appetite-inducing high. Tall, lanky, and vine-like, the sativa plant is often nearly twice the size of a typical indica plant. Sativa produces light, fluffy marijuana buds that take a long time to finish flowering—sometimes almost twice as long as indica.

In the 1960s and '70s, sativa was plentiful in America. The majority of America's cannabis supply came from tropical South American countries where sativas grew in plenty and law enforcement was lax. These strains had names like Colombian Gold, Panama Red, and Acapulco Gold. The Vietnam War also created opportunities to smuggle in another sativa strain, Thai (also called Thai Sticks).

Recent efforts to cater to cannabis enthusiasts' desires for a tasty toke and balanced high have created numerous hybrids that offer both the uplifting, spacey cerebral stimulation while also delivering strong physical effects.

WHICH STRAIN IS RIGHT FOR ME?

The strain you choose depends on the effect you're seeking. Some people love uplifting sativa strains because they may relieve mental ailments such as depression. Other people find that sativa strains increase their creativity. Still others find that sativa can

take the place of pharmaceutical medications for ADHD. While many people relish sativa's energizing effect, others become anxious and/or stressed by sativas; the uplifting high is too much for them.

Pure indica strains have a far more physical result than sativa strains, making users feel relaxed and even slightly Gumby-like (they sometimes experience what's referred to as "couch lock"). People with insomnia and anxiety often find the sedating effect of indicas very helpful. Indicas can also be good for muscle spasms and managing other types of physical pain.

Hybrid strains are a mix of sativa and indica—they can be either an equal mix, or more of one or the other.

Many people who use cannabis find that they like different strains for different aspects of their life. For example, cannabis strains with sedative effects might be great before bedtime, while more stimulating strains could be a good choice for social occasions. And some people find that hybrids offer the best of both worlds. Finding what strain or strains are right for you truly depends on your individual taste and may take some experimentation. However, if you are using cannabis for medical reasons, speak with a professional to determine which strain is right for you.

WHY DIFFERENT STRAINS HAVE UNIQUE TASTES

The different tastes of certain strains of cannabis are a product of controlled breeding programs. Marijuana producers select their best-tasting marijuana plant and breed it with their highest-yielding strain, hoping to create an offspring that will taste great and produce a lot of bud. These breeding programs have created cannabis hybrids that taste dramatically different from one another. Growers give these hybrids names that often reflect specific properties of that hybrid, such as taste, smell, color, or origin. The popular variety Blackberry Kush is an example.

Sativa strains are often considered more tasty than their indica counterparts. This is because indica strains were originally produced mostly for their effects and high yield, rather than for flavor.

THE ROLE OF TERPENES

You don't have to be a "cannaisseur" to know that this herb has a powerful, pungent, one-of-a-kind aroma. A collection of flavor molecules known as terpenes are responsible for cannabis's distinct scent and taste. Terpenes don't only occur in cannabis, however; they are thought to be the most widespread group of natural products on our planet.[7] Trees, plants, and even insects secrete them into the air, spurring a burst of chemical reactions in nearby plants and animals.[8]

Three of the most prevalent flavor terpenes in cannabis include myrcene, pinene, and limonene.[9] As its name suggests, pinene is behind the woody, pine taste found in many marijuana strains.[10] Limonene-heavy strains often have a strong sweet, citrusy aroma.[11] Myrcene, a terpene that's also found in India pale ales, gives cannabis a pungent scent and hops-like flavor.[12]

In the natural world, terpenes serve as a plant's external immune system, producing compounds that ward off harmful parasites, viruses, and bacteria while also attracting pollinators.[13] In humans, terpenes also act as powerful antioxidants, reducing cancer-causing free radicals, protecting cells from damage, and offering antifungal and antibacterial properties.[14, 15]

In marijuana, terpenes work in conjunction with cannabinoids like THC, modifying the plant's psychoactive and medicinal effects.[16] In a way, terpenes act as accents to cannabinoids, slightly coloring the way they interact with your body.

COOKING WITH CANNABIS

It is easier than ever to select cannabis strains strictly by flavor profile. Cannabis growers often selectively breed strains based on cannabinoid and terpene profiles. For example, strains like Blueberry and Blackberry Kush were created specifically for their sweet, fruity, and sometimes smoky tastes and aromas.

Cannabis testing allows us to see exactly what percentage of any given terpene is present in a particular strain sample, along with important information such as the presence of pesticide residue, microorganisms, and molds. All of these factors will impact the flavor and edibility of your cannabis. Ask your supplier for their online testing results. Not only will this tell you whether or not your herb was properly processed, but it can also help you select the best-tasting strain for your dish.

Depending on the strain you use, cannabis can have a very strong flavor. While the use of extractions and modern cooking methods reduce the flavor considerably, another way to tone down its taste is to increase the use of herbs and spices in your dishes. Conversely, you can use fewer herbs and spices if you would like the cannabis flavor to be front and center.

EXTRACTIONS

Cannabis extract is similar to other botanical concentrates, such as almond, anise, and vanilla extracts—except, of course, cannabis extracts can be extremely psychoactive. If you have a high-THC extract, a couple of drops can equal a complete dose. So until you know how your extractions affect you, we recommend you follow our recipes exactly.

There are several different methods of extracting cannabis, ranging from simple, do-it-yourself stovetop productions to extractions that are best left to professionals with access to the correct safety and processing equipment. Home cannabis extractions usually take the form of cannabis-infused fats, most commonly butter or oil. The THC in cannabis is almost entirely insoluble in water, but is very soluble in fat. Because of this, heating cannabis in butter or oil breaks down the THC and allows it to bind to the fat, creating an easy vehicle for introducing activated, terpene-rich cannabis into any meal or dish.

A few common at-home extractions include:

Cannabutter: Whether you prefer clarified ghee in a curry or some herbal butter to pair with your morning toast and jam, cannabis-infused butter is one of the most versatile extractions you can make. See the recipe on page 29.

Canna-olive oil: For use in everything from salad dressings to sauces to baked goods, marijuana-infused olive oil is a must-have when it comes to cannabis cooking. While any olive oil works for extractions, we recommend using extra-virgin olive oil for dishes where we want the taste of the oil to shine through, such as pastas and salads. See the recipe on page 28.

Canna-coconut oil: Perfect for use in sautés and stir-fries that require high heat, and as a filler for homemade THC or CBD capsules, infused coconut oil also makes an excellent balm for dry skin. See the recipe on page 28.

DECARBOXYLATION

To bring out the full flavor potential of herbs and spices, many cooks toast them before cooking. The same principle applies to cannabis. When you expose this herb to even, gentle heat by toasting it in an oven, simmering it in a fat, or holding it to a flame, its flavor compounds and its THC begin to denature. Strong aromas erupt, creating an intricate palette of taste and scent and unlocking marijuana's psychoactive effects. This process is called decarboxylation (or "decarbing").

To put it another way, without decarboxylation, cannabis is just a plain and simple herb. Thorough toasting transforms its THC from inactive organic material into the psychoactive we know and love.

Decarboxylation is a simple process with just a few steps:

1. Preheat the oven to 240°F.
2. Break up cannabis flowers and buds into smaller pieces with your hands. We use one ounce, but you can elect to do more or less.
3. Put the pieces in one layer on a rimmed baking sheet. Make sure the pan is the correct size so there is not empty space on the pan.
4. Bake the cannabis for 30 to 40 minutes, stirring every 10 minutes so that it toasts evenly.
5. When the cannabis is darker in color, a light to medium brown, and has dried out, remove the baking sheet and allow the cannabis to cool. It will be crumbly.
6. In a food processor, pulse the cannabis until it is coarsely ground (you don't want a superfine powder). Store it in an airtight container and use as needed to make extractions (see recipes on page 28).

DOSING

Cannabis affects everyone in a different way (and different varieties have different strengths), so finding how much cannabis is right for you will take some experimentation on your part. The amount of THC can vary per bud, sometimes wildly. That said, here are some guidelines:

1. For the purpose of standardizing dosing, the recipes in this book all use cannabis that tests at 12 percent THC. A single serving size for any given recipe contains a dose of 10 milligrams of THC (equivalent to 1 teaspoon of cannabutter or cannaoil). In our tests, this dose was enough for occasional cannabis users to feel significant psychoactivity.
2. If you are new to cannabis or edibles, we recommend starting with half a serving size or even less for your first few times until you better understand how the THC level affects you. Keep in mind that the potency of different strains can vary widely, so account for variability when dosing and be conservative.
3. Edibles with a higher fat content will generally have a longer-lasting effect compared to edibles with a high sugar content, which will pass through your system more quickly.
4. Cannabis consumed orally can affect the body much more strongly than cannabis consumed by smoking or vaping. In addition to that, it can take anywhere from 45 minutes to 5 hours (or even longer) to feel the effects of cannabis consumed in edible form. It is impossible to know how edibles will affect you until you try them (body weight seems to have nothing to do with the strength of the effect), so be cautious and responsible. Until you know how cannabis

affects you, you should try edibles on a full stomach, or eat something without cannabis in it along with your edible.

5. Until you find the dose that is right for you, we also recommend consuming an edible and then waiting several hours (or even overnight) for the effects to kick in. What often happens is that people don't feel the effects of cannabis in an hour or so, and then, thinking it hasn't worked, they ingest more, only to become unpleasantly stoned later.

6. Finally, we suggest you try edibles for the first time or first few times while you are at home, and do so over a weekend or during another long stretch of time when you won't need to be working or driving.

7. The Marijuana Policy Project has put together an excellent website that we recommend to anyone interested in consuming edibles: www.consumeresponsibly.org.

SOME NOTES ON THE RECIPES

Choosing an Oil
Some recipes call for specific types of cannaoil, such as canna-olive oil or canna-coconut oil. In those cases, we chose a particular oil because it affects the taste of the final dish. Where it's not specified, you can use any type of cannaoil you have on hand.

Cooking over Low Heat
THC can degrade at high heat—as a result, the recipes in this book all call for low to medium heat. Our motto when cooking with cannabutter or cannaoil is "low and slow."

When recipes require the use of an oven, the temperature never exceeds 340°F. In our recipe testing, we found that this was the highest temperature at which THC's potency could be preserved. To make sure you can replicate this in your own kitchen, you may wish to invest in an oven thermometer to calibrate the temperature of your oven.

Mixing Thoroughly
This step is the most important to ensure even distribution of THC throughout the dish. When the recipe calls for adding the cannaoil or cannabutter, mix for at least 1 full minute—2 is even better. Scrape down the sides of the bowl, if needed, to get the last bits.

Serving Sizes
Many recipes have serving sizes, but some do not. Every recipe does state how many servings it makes, so for the recipes without serving sizes, use this as a guideline. For example, you can eyeball the Spaghetti with Arugula Pesto (page 131) once you've dished it out on four plates to ascertain that all the servings are equal.

Remember that each teaspoon of cannabutter or cannaoil in the recipe equates to 10 milligrams of THC, a recommended serving size for an experienced cannabis user. Follow your own tolerance to determine whether you are able to consume a whole serving.

MAKING CANNAOIL AND CANNABUTTER

CANNAOIL

MAKES:
6 cups

SERVING SIZE:
1 teaspoon

DIFFICULTY:
Easy

You can use any type of cooking oil to make cannaoil, even a blend of two or more oils. A good rule of thumb is to use the oils you already employ in your cooking, but some recipes in this book call specifically for canna-olive oil, canna-vegetable oil, and canna-coconut oil. We use GMO-free oils wherever we can.

Note that the finished cannaoil will have a green tinge to it because of the cannabis. Stored in a cool, dark place, cannaoil will keep for up to six months.

EQUIPMENT NEEDED

Large saucepan/pot

Whisk

Large glass bowl

Strainer or sieve that fits in the glass bowl

Cheesecloth

Spatula

Lidded glass jar (to store the finished cannaoil)

INGREDIENTS

6 cups cooking oil of your choice (such as olive, coconut, grape seed, sunflower, canola, or a mixture)

1 ounce decarboxylated, ground cannabis buds, or 2 ounces decarboxylated dried, ground, and trimmed cannabis leaf (see "Decarboxylation" on page 26)

PROCEDURE

1. In a large saucepan, slowly heat the oil over low heat.
2. Whisk in the cannabis.
3. Cook for 3 hours, stirring every 30 minutes. Occasional bubbles in the mixture are okay, but do not let it boil.
4. While the oil cooks, line a strainer or sieve with cheesecloth and place it over a large glass bowl.
5. After 3 hours, pour the oil through the cheesecloth into the bowl. Press down on the cannabis with a spatula to extract all the oil. Discard the cheesecloth.
6. Transfer the oil to a glass jar with a lid and store it in a cool, dark place.

CANNABUTTER

When you're making cannabutter, the key thing to remember is "low and slow"—infusing the butter over low heat for several hours, never letting it boil, allows for full activation of the THC without scorching the herb. You can use any kind of unsalted butter you like, though we find that using high-quality butter provides a better taste. High-quality butter has less water, so you will get a higher yield.

Note that the finished butter will have a green tinge to it because of the cannabis. Cannabutter will keep in the fridge for several weeks and in the freezer for up to six months.

MAKES:
1 pound

SERVING SIZE:
1 teaspoon

DIFFICULTY:
Intermediate

EQUIPMENT NEEDED

Large saucepan/pot

Whisk

Large glass bowl

Strainer or sieve that fits in the glass bowl

Cheesecloth

Spatula

Plastic wrap

Butter knife

Lidded glass jar (to store the finished cannabutter)

INGREDIENTS

1 pound unsalted butter

2 cups water

1 ounce decarboxylated, ground cannabis buds, or 2 ounces decarboxylated dried, ground, and trimmed cannabis leaf (see "Decarboxylation" on page 26)

PROCEDURE

1. In a large saucepan, bring the butter and water to a rapid simmer (just below a boil—the liquid will be active, with small bubbles consistently rising to the surface) over medium heat until the butter melts.
2. Whisk in the cannabis.
3. Reduce the heat to low and bring the mixture to a slow simmer (there will be very little movement in the liquid, with small bubbles occasionally rising to the surface). Do not let the mixture boil.
4. Cook for 5 hours, stirring every 90 minutes or so. Add additional warm water if needed (you don't want all the water to boil off).
5. While the butter cooks, line a strainer or sieve with cheesecloth and place it over a large glass bowl.
6. After 5 hours, pour the butter slowly through the cheesecloth into the bowl. Press down on the cannabis with a spatula to extract all the butter.
7. Fold the cheesecloth, and use the spatula to push any remaining cannabutter into the bowl. Discard the cheesecloth.
8. Cover the bowl with plastic wrap and refrigerate it for at least 3 hours (overnight is better). The mixture will separate into solid butter and liquid water.
9. Remove the butter from the fridge, discard the water, and slide a butter knife around the edges to remove the cannabutter from the bowl.
10. Transfer the butter to a glass jar with a lid and store it in the fridge or freezer.

COMPOUND CANNABUTTERS

MAKES:

1¼–1½ cups

SERVING SIZE:

1 teaspoon

DIFFICULTY:

Easy

Compound butters are butters that have been flavored with ingredients such as fresh or dried herbs, citrus zest, spices, pickles, sweet ingredients, or cheeses. To make them, the ingredients of choice are finely minced or chopped and mixed into softened butter, which is then rolled into a cylindrical or log shape, and chilled or frozen. The butter is sliced and served as a spread or topping on foods—added to finished steaks, chops, fish, vegetable dishes, pastas, and burgers, for example, or used as a sweet flourish in breakfast or dessert recipes. Compound cannabutters can be refrigerated for one week or frozen for four weeks without losing their potency.

INGREDIENTS

Garlic-Herb Cannabutter:
1 cup cannabutter

½ cup finely chopped fresh parsley

1½ teaspoons sea salt

1 teaspoon coarsely ground fresh black pepper

1 teaspoon garlic powder

1 teaspoon onion powder

Raspberry-Mint Cannabutter:
1 cup cannabutter

½ pint fresh raspberries, mashed

¼ cup confectioners' sugar

2 tablespoons chopped fresh mint

⅛ teaspoon mint extract

Pinch of sea salt

Rémoulade Cannabutter:
1 cup cannabutter

1½ tablespoons dehydrated onion

¼ cup green bell pepper, seeded and finely diced

1 tablespoon ketchup

2 teaspoons olive oil

2 teaspoons prepared fresh horseradish

1 to 3 teaspoons (depending on heat level desired) Louisiana hot sauce

1 teaspoon Worcestershire sauce

1½ teaspoons celery salt

Kosher salt and finely ground fresh black pepper, to taste

PROCEDURE

1. Choose a flavor for your compound cannabutter. At left are ingredients lists for three versions of compound cannabutter, but we encourage you to experiment and develop your own as well. For the best flavor, always use fresh (rather than dried or bottled) ingredients, such as herbs and citrus juices.

2. Bring your cannabutter to room temperature and blend in additional ingredients. This can be done by hand (with a fork or spoon) or in a food processor. To ensure even distribution, mix the butter for at least 1 to 2 minutes. If you use a food processor, be sure not to overmix (you don't want to heat the butter up too much).

3. Once the butter is thoroughly blended, transfer it to a piece of parchment paper or plastic wrap. Roll the butter into a log and wrap it tightly. Put it in a freezer zip-top bag before storing it in the fridge or freezer. (If it's not properly stored, butter can absorb flavors that may be lingering in your fridge or freezer.)

CHEFS' NOTE

Cannabutters should not be heated to a high temperature, because a large percentage of the THC will evaporate, resulting in a bitter-tasting, minimally medicated edible. In the recipes in this book, compound cannabutters are usually added at the very end of a recipe, so there is little danger of them overheating.

Dips and
Appetizers

SPICY SPINACH, KALE, AND ARTICHOKE DIP

This dip, with its crunchy topping and creamy interior, is a proven crowd-pleaser. If you like things spicier, add a few more tablespoons of pickled jalapeños (available at Latin American markets or online) before baking, or lightly sprinkle red pepper flakes over the top of the baked dip. Serve this with chips, crudités, or toast.

MAKES:

4 cups

SERVING SIZE:

¹⁄₃ cup

DIFFICULTY:

Easy

INGREDIENTS

¼ cup cannabutter

1 tablespoon chopped garlic

8 ounces cream cheese, softened

1¼ cups freshly grated Parmesan cheese, ¼ cup reserved for topping

²⁄₃ cup low-fat sour cream

¼ cup mayonnaise

¾ cup chopped canned, jarred, or frozen artichoke hearts (thawed and drained if frozen)

2 tablespoons chopped pickled jalapeños

½ teaspoon salt (kosher or sea)

½ teaspoon freshly ground black pepper

Pinch of ground nutmeg

1 cup finely chopped fresh kale leaves (any variety), stems discarded

1 cup frozen spinach, thawed and drained

¼ cup plain bread crumbs

PROCEDURE

1. Preheat the oven to 325°F.
2. In a small saucepan, melt the cannabutter over low heat.
3. When the butter has melted, add the garlic and cook for 2 minutes, until it has colored slightly. Remove the pan from the heat and let the garlic butter cool.
4. In a large bowl, stir together the cream cheese, 1 cup of the Parmesan, sour cream, mayonnaise, artichokes, jalapeños, salt, pepper, and nutmeg.
5. Stir in the kale and spinach.
6. Add the cooled garlic butter and mix thoroughly.
7. Pour the dip into an oven-safe dish (1 quart) and top with the bread crumbs and reserved Parmesan.
8. Bake until the top is golden brown, about 20 minutes.

BLACK BEAN DIP

With the fresh taste of lime, tomato, and cilantro, this is not your run-of-the-mill bean dip. Made with canned beans, it's a quick, easy, and delicious appetizer. Serve it with warm blue and white corn tortilla chips or vegetable crudités.

MAKES:

3 cups

SERVING SIZE:

⅓ cup

DIFFICULTY:

Easy

INGREDIENTS

3 cups unsalted black beans (from two 15-ounce cans), drained and rinsed

2 tablespoons chopped green chilies (fresh or canned)

2 teaspoons chopped garlic

1 tablespoon plus 2 teaspoons tomato paste

1 teaspoon ketchup

Juice of 1 lime

¾ teaspoon ground cumin

¾ teaspoon salt (kosher or sea)

½ teaspoon freshly ground black pepper

¼ teaspoon chili powder

¼ teaspoon cayenne pepper

3 tablespoons cannaoil

2 green onions (white and green parts), chopped

1 Roma tomato, seeded and chopped

¼ cup chopped fresh cilantro leaves

Crumbled queso fresco (optional)

PROCEDURE

1. In the bowl of a food processor fitted with a metal blade, pulse the beans, chilies, garlic, tomato paste, ketchup, lime juice, cumin, salt, black pepper, chili powder, and cayenne until smooth and thoroughly combined, scraping the sides of the bowl as needed.

2. With the machine running, add the cannaoil in a steady stream through the feed tube. Blend for 1 minute to incorporate the oil.

3. Transfer the dip to a serving bowl and top with the green onions, tomato, cilantro, and queso fresco, if using.

CHEFS' NOTES

This spread works great as a substitute for mayonnaise on any sandwich.

WHITE BEAN CURRY DIP

Curry lovers, this dip is for you. It's irresistible spread on warm toasted naan (our favorite is garlic naan) and topped with sliced radishes.

MAKES:

3 cups

SERVING SIZE:

⅓ cup

DIFFICULTY:

Easy

INGREDIENTS

2 (15-ounce) cans cannellini beans, drained and rinsed

1 large or 2 medium garlic cloves, finely chopped

1¼ teaspoons curry powder

½ teaspoon kosher salt

¼ teaspoon ground cumin

¼ teaspoon sweet paprika

¼ teaspoon white pepper

3 tablespoons cannaoil

1 tablespoon grape-seed or olive oil

1 tablespoon freshly squeezed lemon juice

1 tablespoon chopped fresh parsley, for garnish

Olive oil, for garnish

PROCEDURE

1. In the bowl of a food processor fitted with a metal blade, pulse the beans, garlic, curry powder, salt, cumin, paprika, and white pepper until smooth and thoroughly combined, scraping the sides of the bowl as needed.
2. In a measuring cup with a spout, combine the cannaoil, grape-seed oil, and lemon juice.
3. With the machine running, add the cannaoil mixture in a steady stream through the feed tube, scraping the cup to ensure no oil is left. Blend for 1 minute to incorporate the oil.
4. Transfer the dip to a serving bowl and top with the parsley and a drizzle of olive oil.

CARAMELIZED ONION DIP WITH TOMATO TOASTS

MAKES:

3 cups

SERVING SIZE:

¼ cup

DIFFICULTY:

Intermediate

Melissa's onion dip puts others to shame. And while it takes a little while to make, it's worth the effort. The combination of flavors is really highlighted by the roasted garlic—sometimes we roast an extra head and keep it in the fridge in butter or oil. It's a delicious spread in its own right.

INGREDIENTS

For the dip:
1 head garlic

²/₃ cup olive oil, plus more
for brushing the garlic

2 tablespoons unsalted butter

2 cups finely diced red onion

2 cups finely diced
sweet white onion

2 tablespoons sugar

¼ cup cannabutter

¼ cup mayonnaise made
with olive oil

1 teaspoon sherry vinegar

1 tablespoon finely
chopped fresh parsley

1 tablespoon minced fresh
rosemary

1 tablespoon minced fresh chives

3 tablespoons freshly grated
Parmesan cheese, plus more for
dusting the dip

2 tablespoons freshly grated
Romano cheese

Kosher salt and freshly ground
black pepper, to taste

For the toasts:
1 baguette

3 Roma tomatoes,
halved lengthwise

PROCEDURE

Make the dip:

1. Preheat the oven to 400°F. Slice the garlic head in half crosswise to expose the raw cloves. Brush the exposed cloves with olive oil. Wrap the halves loosely in aluminum foil with the clove side up, and put them in an ovenproof pan.

2. Roast the garlic until it's tender, about 30 minutes. Set it aside to cool. Once the garlic is cool enough to handle, squeeze the heads to push the roasted garlic from the skins into a bowl. Discard the skins.

3. In a large skillet, heat the ²/₃ cup olive oil and butter over medium heat.

4. Add the roasted garlic, red onion, and white onion. Cook the onions until they are softened and beginning to brown, 7 to 9 minutes.

5. Add the sugar and cook, stirring periodically so the onions do not stick to the pan, until they are a rich deep-brown color, 20 to 25 minutes.

6. Turn the heat off and swirl in the cannabutter until melted. Set the mixture aside to cool to room temperature.

7. When the onion mixture has cooled, transfer it to a large bowl, and add the mayonnaise, vinegar, parsley, rosemary, chives, Parmesan, Romano, salt, and pepper.

8. Refrigerate the mixture for at least 2 hours to allow the flavors to come together.

9. Just before serving, preheat the oven to 300°F. Put the dip in an ovenproof pie plate and sprinkle with a dusting of Parmesan.

Make the toasts:

10. Heat the dip and baguette until the dip is warmed through and the bread is crisp, 5 to 7 minutes.

11. Slice the baguette into thin slices on the diagonal.

12. Rub each slice with the halved tomatoes and serve alongside the dip.

CHEFS' NOTE
Leftover dip makes a great sandwich topper or pasta addition,
or spread it between two tortillas with cheddar cheese.

HUMMUS

MAKES:

1½ cups

SERVING SIZE:

¼ cup

DIFFICULTY:

Easy

There are many flavors of hummus available these days, but we still think the original is best—with cannabis, of course. Using canned beans makes it easy to whip up, and it's a great staple to have in the fridge for late-night munchies. It's fantastic with pita chips or veggies, or as a spread on sandwiches. Tahini is sesame seed paste and can be found in most grocery stores.

INGREDIENTS

1 tablespoon water

1 medium garlic clove, coarsely chopped

¼ cup tahini

1 tablespoon freshly squeezed lemon juice

1 (15-ounce) can chickpeas, drained and rinsed

2 tablespoons cannaoil

1 teaspoon freshly grated lemon zest

¼ teaspoon smoked sweet paprika

¼ teaspoon ground turmeric

Salt (kosher or sea) and freshly ground black pepper, to taste

PROCEDURE

1. In the bowl of a food processor fitted with a metal blade, pulse the water, garlic, tahini, and lemon juice to a smooth paste.
2. Add half of the chickpeas and pulse to combine. Scrape down the sides of the bowl before adding the remaining chickpeas.
3. With the machine running, add the cannaoil in a steady stream through the feed tube. Blend until the hummus reaches your desired consistency.
4. Add the zest, paprika, turmeric, salt, and pepper and pulse briefly to combine.

CHEFS' NOTE

If you're not a fan of hummus, substitute black beans for the chickpeas and cumin for the turmeric.
Stir in chopped fresh cilantro and diced tomatoes and serve with tortilla chips.

GUACAMOLE

Avocados have tremendous health benefits and they also taste great, especially when made into guacamole. To keep your guac from turning brown, drizzle it with citrus juice and press plastic wrap snugly into its surface (this limits the oxygen exposure that leads to browning). We like our guacamole chunky, so we mash the avocado only enough to break it up a bit, but you can make yours as smooth as you like.

INGREDIENTS

2 large ripe avocados, peeled and seeded

Juice of 2 medium limes

4 teaspoons cannaoil

½ small red onion, diced

¼ cup finely chopped cilantro leaves

½ teaspoon kosher salt

1 small tomato, seeded and chopped (optional)

PROCEDURE

1. In a medium bowl, mash the avocado.
2. Add all the other ingredients and mix thoroughly.

MAKES:

2 cups

SERVES:

4

SERVING SIZE:

½ cup

DIFFICULTY:

Easy

QUESO SAUCE

When you taste made-from-scratch queso sauce, you may never buy the jarred kind again. While we love this sauce with tortilla chips, we've been known to dip just about anything in it.

MAKES:

4 cups

SERVING SIZE:

²/₃ cup

DIFFICULTY:

Easy

INGREDIENTS

2 cups whole milk

1 cup heavy cream

2 tablespoons cannabutter

1 tablespoon butter

3 tablespoons all-purpose flour

2 cups freshly grated sharp cheddar cheese

½ cup freshly grated pepper Jack cheese

¼ cup freshly grated Parmesan cheese

4 ounces cream cheese, cubed, at room temperature

½ teaspoon salt (kosher or sea)

½ teaspoon freshly ground black pepper

Cayenne pepper, to taste

PROCEDURE

1. In a small saucepan, heat the milk and heavy cream over low heat until it is warm to the touch. Remove the pan from the heat and set it aside.
2. In a heavy saucepan, melt the cannabutter and butter over medium-low heat. Whisk in the flour (the mixture should resemble wet sand). Continue to cook for 2 minutes, whisking constantly.
3. Gradually whisk in half of the warm milk mixture, stirring until all the flour lumps are gone and the sauce is smooth and creamy. Whisk in the remaining milk mixture, and cook until the sauce thickens enough to coat the back of a spoon, 7 to 9 minutes.
4. Add the cheddar, pepper Jack, and Parmesan ½ cup at a time, whisking constantly, until all the cheese has melted. Add the cream cheese a few cubes at a time, whisking constantly and waiting until each portion has melted before adding more.
5. Season with salt, pepper, and a pinch of cayenne.

CHEFS' NOTES

For a spicy kick, add diced pickled jalapeños and a few splashes of your favorite hot sauce.

Adding diced tomatoes and chopped cilantro gives the sauce a fresh note.

NACHOS WITH CHEDDAR CHEESE SAUCE

Back in the day, we made nachos with shredded cheese. It got the job done, but once we started using this cheddar cheese sauce, we've never looked back (although sometimes we also garnish the nachos with shredded cheese, just to gild the lily).

INGREDIENTS

3 cups tortilla chips

3 green onions (white and green parts), chopped

1 small tomato, seeded and chopped

1 cup Cheddar Cheese Sauce (recipe below)

PROCEDURE

1. Preheat the oven to 325°F.
2. Put the chips on a baking sheet and bake until light golden brown, 8 to 10 minutes.
3. Transfer the chips to a serving platter.
4. Top with the green onions and tomato.
5. Pour the cheese sauce over chips and serve immediately.

CHEDDAR CHEESE SAUCE

This sauce is unbeatable on nachos, but it also has a myriad of other uses—which is good, because the recipe makes more than you'll need for the nachos. We like to pour it on top of potato hash and a sunny-side-up egg for a weekend breakfast, or add it to a baked potato loaded with fresh vegetables for a quick and easy late-night snack. If you don't have white pepper, black pepper works just as well.

INGREDIENTS

2 tablespoons butter

8 teaspoons cannabutter

3 tablespoons all-purpose flour

½ teaspoon kosher salt

½ teaspoon white pepper

1 cup (whole or 2 percent) milk

1 cup heavy cream

2 ounces cream cheese, slightly softened

1½ cups freshly grated sharp cheddar

Pinch of ground nutmeg

PROCEDURE

1. In a medium saucepan, melt the butter and cannabutter over low heat. Whisk in the flour, salt, and white pepper and cook for several minutes, stirring, to remove the raw flour taste.
2. Slowly pour in the milk and cream, stirring constantly; this ensures a smooth and creamy consistency. Once the milk and cream have been added, add the cream cheese in three or four pieces, whisking between each addition.
3. Continue to cook the sauce over medium-low heat until it is thick enough to coat the back of a spoon, 7 to 10 minutes.
4. Reduce the heat to low and add the cheddar a ½ cup at a time, whisking between each addition, 5 to 6 minutes.
5. Remove the pan from the heat, stir in the nutmeg, and serve immediately.

MAKES:
2 cups

SERVING SIZE:
¼ cup

DIFFICULTY:
Medium

CHEFS' NOTES

Add crumbled cooked sausage, bacon, or Turkey Meatballs (page 145) for a heartier dish.

CHORIZO-GOAT CHEESE QUESADILLAS

A quesadilla can be so much more than just melted cheese in a tortilla. Our version pairs spicy chorizo with the creaminess and tang of goat cheese.

MAKES:
2 servings

SERVING SIZE:
½ quesadilla

DIFFICULTY:
Easy

INGREDIENTS

1 tablespoon olive oil

2 green onions (white and green parts), chopped

1 link chorizo, removed from the casing and crumbled, or ¼ cup bulk chorizo

¼ cup creamy goat cheese

2 teaspoons cannaoil

2 (6-inch) flour tortillas

Sour cream, for serving (optional)

Salsa, for serving (optional)

PROCEDURE

1. In a medium skillet, heat the olive oil over medium heat.
2. Add the green onions and chorizo, breaking the sausage up with a spoon into small pieces. Sauté until the onions are tender and all the pink has disappeared from the meat.
3. In a medium bowl, stir together the goat cheese and cannaoil. Add the chorizo mixture and mix thoroughly. Don't wash the skillet.
4. In the same skillet, heat one of the tortillas.
5. Spread the filling across one tortilla, leaving a ¼-inch border around the edges, and place the second tortilla on top.
6. Cook the quesadilla, turning once, until golden brown, 5 to 7 minutes total.
7. Let the quesadilla rest for a few minutes before cutting it in half and serving it with the sour cream and salsa, if using.

GARLIC BREAD

MAKES:

16 slices

SERVING SIZE:

1 slice

DIFFICULTY:

Easy

Garlic bread is one of the tastiest things on earth. Laurie ate a particularly delectable version at Yellow Fingers, a New York City restaurant. This is our take on that recipe. The bread is baked twice, which takes a little more time, but the resulting texture and taste are unbeatable.

INGREDIENTS

½ cup (1 stick) butter, softened

2 tablespoons plus 2 teaspoons cannabutter, softened

4 garlic cloves, minced

½ teaspoon kosher salt

2 tablespoons minced fresh parsley (optional)

1 baguette, sliced lengthwise

PROCEDURE

1. Put a rack in the middle of the oven and set it to broil. Line a baking sheet with aluminum foil and set it aside.
2. In a small bowl, combine the butter, cannabutter, garlic, salt, and parsley, if using.
3. Put the bread on the prepared baking sheet cut side up and broil until it is medium golden brown, anywhere from 2 to 5 minutes.
4. Remove the bread from the oven and immediately slather it with the butter mixture.
5. Reduce the oven temperature to 340°F.
6. Wrap the bread in aluminum foil and bake it for 10 minutes.
7. Carefully open the aluminum foil (it will be hot) and slice each half of the baguette into 8 pieces. Serve immediately.

CHEFS' NOTE

For an even more decadent garlic bread, sprinkle ⅓ cup freshly grated Parmesan cheese on top before wrapping the bread and baking.

ROASTED CHERRY TOMATO BRUSCHETTA

MAKES:

8 bruschetta

SERVING SIZE:

2 bruschetta

DIFFICULTY:

Easy

Bruschetta is a perfect way to use leftover bread and showcase foods at their peak of freshness. Its most common incarnation involves fresh tomatoes and basil, but we upped the ante with a combination of roasted tomatoes, yellow peppers, and scallions. Roasting the tomatoes adds a level of complexity and is also a way to make not-so-perfect specimens taste great. Using high-quality bread makes all the difference.

INGREDIENTS

8 thick slices baguette

3 garlic cloves, peeled
(2 left whole, 1 minced)

4 teaspoons canna-olive oil

2 cups cherry tomatoes

½ yellow pepper, cut in small strips

3 green onions (white and green parts), cut into 1-inch pieces

2 tablespoons olive oil

Coarse salt (kosher or sea) and freshly ground black pepper, to taste

PROCEDURE

1. Preheat the oven to 325°F.
2. Put the bread slices on a baking sheet and toast them, about 5 to 7 minutes.
3. Remove the bread from the oven and, while it's still warm, rub one side of each slice with the 2 whole garlic cloves. Drizzle or brush the slices with the cannaoil.
4. On a rimmed baking sheet, toss the minced garlic, tomatoes, peppers, and green onions with the olive oil. Bake until the tomatoes have lost their shape and the scallions have started to turn golden brown, about 15 minutes.
5. Divide the tomato mixture among the bread slices and sprinkle with salt and pepper.

CHEFS' NOTE
Grilling the bread instead of toasting it in the oven is an easy way to add an extra layer of flavor.

BRUSCHETTA WITH RICOTTA AND PEAS

Ricotta is a totally underutilized cheese. It's spreadable and creamy, with a subtle flavor, and its texture pairs nicely with the crunch of toasted bread and the sweetness of peas in this recipe.

MAKES:

8 bruschetta

SERVING SIZE:

2 bruschetta

DIFFICULTY:

Easy

INGREDIENTS

8 slices peasant bread, lightly toasted

4 teaspoons canna-olive oil

1 cup ricotta cheese

3 tablespoons plus 2 teaspoons olive oil, divided

2 tablespoons chopped onion or green onion

½ cup peas, fresh or frozen (thawed, if frozen)

Salt (kosher or sea) and freshly ground black pepper, to taste

PROCEDURE

1. Drizzle or brush the toasted bread with the canna-olive oil, using ½ teaspoon per slice.
2. Spread 2 tablespoons of ricotta on each slice.
3. In a small skillet, heat 1 tablespoon of the olive oil. Add the onions and sauté until they wilt slightly, 3 to 4 minutes.
4. Add the peas and sauté until they soften and are no longer vibrant green, 3 to 4 minutes more.
5. Divide the pea mixture among the bread slices.
6. Drizzle each slice with 1 teaspoon of the remaining olive oil and sprinkle with salt and pepper.

DEVILS ON HORSEBACK
(BACON-WRAPPED DATES)

This appetizer is a throwback to the 1970s, but it's still a hit today. Dates have fabulous flavor, and when they're stuffed with cannabutter and goat cheese and wrapped in bacon, you could enter them in the appetizer hall of fame.

MAKES:
16 wrapped dates

SERVING SIZE:
4 dates

DIFFICULTY:
Easy

INGREDIENTS

16 pitted dates

2 tablespoons goat cheese

4 teaspoons cannabutter

8 strips bacon, cut in half crosswise

PROCEDURE

1. Preheat the oven to 325°F.
2. With a small knife, make a slit in each date and spread it open.
3. In a small bowl, thoroughly combine the goat cheese with the cannabutter.
4. Divide the mixture among the dates, pressing it into the center and closing the dates after filling.
5. Wrap a bacon slice around each stuffed date.
6. Put the dates, bacon seam down, on a baking sheet.
7. Bake until the bacon is crisp, about 10 minutes.

CHEFS' NOTES

Try blue cheese instead of goat cheese.

For a crunchier version, add some toasted walnuts or pecans to the cheese-butter mixture before wrapping the dates. Be sure to let your guests know—otherwise they might think they've just chomped down on the date's pit!

DUMPLINGS WITH ASIAN DIPPING SAUCE

MAKES:

6 servings

SERVING SIZE:

¼ cup

DIFFICULTY:

Easy

There are plenty of excellent packaged frozen dumplings on the market, so there's no need to make them from scratch. The accompanying dipping sauce comes together quickly and really makes the meal.

INGREDIENTS

2 tablespoons cannaoil

1 package of your favorite frozen Asian-style dumplings

½ cup creamy peanut butter

2 tablespoons low-sodium soy sauce

1 tablespoon packed light brown sugar

1 tablespoon freshly squeezed lemon juice

½ teaspoon minced garlic

Pinch of red pepper flakes

PROCEDURE

1. Heat the cannaoil in a large nonstick lidded skillet over medium heat. Place the dumplings flat side down and cook on one side until light golden brown. Turn and cook on the other side until light golden brown, about 8-10 minutes total. Add enough water to cover the bottom quarter of the dumplings, and cover the pan. Cook, covered, for 7 minutes. Remove the cover, allowing the water to evaporate, and cook the dumplings, turning them a few times, until they are golden brown all over and crisped, about another 6-9 minutes.
2. While the dumplings cook, prepare the dipping sauce: in a medium bowl, thoroughly combine the remaining ingredients.
3. Serve the dumplings warm alongside the sauce.

STUFFED MUSHROOMS THREE WAYS

Stuffed mushrooms are beautiful things. We love them so much, we're offering you three variations. To clean the mushrooms before stuffing them, rub them gently with a damp paper towel to remove any dirt—if you run them under water, they'll get soggy and be less flavorful.

ITALIAN-STYLE STUFFED MUSHROOMS

This is the classic recipe. The filling transforms in the oven into luscious cheesy goodness.
Use leftover filling to stuff peppers or fill an omelet.

INGREDIENTS

16 extra-large white button mushrooms, cleaned

2 tablespoons olive oil, plus extra for coating mushrooms

Salt (kosher or sea) and freshly ground black pepper, to taste

½ cup diced shallots

2 garlic cloves, minced

¾ pound ground spicy sausage of your choice

⅔ cup Italian bread crumbs

3 ounces Neufchâtel cheese, at room temperature

1 ounce mascarpone cheese, at room temperature

2 tablespoons plus 2 teaspoons canna-olive oil

⅓ cup freshly grated Parmesan cheese

PROCEDURE

1. Preheat the oven to 325°F.
2. Prepare the mushrooms: Remove and finely chop the stems, and set them aside. Lightly coat each mushroom with olive oil, sprinkle them with salt and pepper, and lay them cap side up on a baking sheet.
3. In a medium skillet, heat the olive oil over medium heat. Add the shallots and garlic and cook until the shallots are translucent, 4 to 6 minutes. Remove the shallots and garlic to a plate.
4. Add the sausage and cook, breaking it up with a spoon into small pieces, until all the pink has disappeared, 4 to 5 minutes.
5. Add the chopped mushroom stems, along with the cooked shallots and garlic, and cook until the stems are tender, 2 to 3 minutes more.
6. Remove the skillet from the heat and stir in the bread crumbs, Neufchâtel, and mascarpone until the cheese has melted and has been distributed throughout.
7. Stir in the cannaoil, mixing thoroughly for 2 minutes.
8. Fill each mushroom cap with 1½ tablespoons of the sausage mixture. Top with the Parmesan, dividing it among the caps. You will have filling left over.
9. Bake the mushrooms until they are tender and the cheese has browned, about 20 minutes.

MAKES:
16 stuffed mushrooms

SERVING SIZE:
2 mushrooms

DIFFICULTY:
Intermediate

CHEFS' NOTE

Other ways to use leftover filling: Use it in an omelet the next morning, or spread it on toast and pop it under the broiler for 3–5 minutes.

SPANISH-STYLE STUFFED MUSHROOMS

These mushrooms are scrumptious on their own, but they're even better served with an easy dipping sauce of ½ cup sour cream, the juice of one lime, and salt and pepper to taste..

INGREDIENTS

16 extra-large white button mushrooms, cleaned

2 tablespoons olive oil, plus extra for coating mushrooms

Salt (kosher or sea) and freshly ground black pepper, to taste

¾ pound chorizo sausage (removed from casing if in links)

½ cup diced green onion (white and green parts)

2 garlic cloves, minced

½ small jalapeño, seeded and finely chopped

2 tablespoons plus 2 teaspoons canna-olive oil

1 Roma tomato, seeded and finely chopped

²/₃ cup panko bread crumbs

3 ounces Neufchâtel cheese, at room temperature

¹/₃ cup cotija cheese, at room temperature

¼ cup chopped cilantro, for garnish

PROCEDURE

1. Prepare the mushrooms as in steps 1–2 on page 63.
2. In a medium skillet, heat the olive oil over medium heat. Add the sausage, and cook, breaking it up with a spoon into small pieces, until all the pink has disappeared, 4 to 5 minutes.
3. Add the chopped mushroom stems, green onion, garlic, and jalapeño and cook until the stems are tender, 2 to 3 minutes more.
4. Remove the skillet from the heat and stir in the cannaoil, mixing thoroughly for 2 minutes.
5. Stir in the tomato, bread crumbs, Neufchâtel, cotija, and a pinch of salt and pepper.
6. Fill the mushroom caps with 1½ tablespoons each of the sausage mixture.
7. Bake the mushrooms until they are tender and the filling is golden brown on top, about 20 minutes.
8. Sprinkle with the cilantro and serve.

MAKES:
16 stuffed mushrooms

SERVING SIZE:
2 mushrooms

DIFFICULTY:
Intermediate

THANKSGIVING-STYLE STUFFED MUSHROOMS

*Serve these topped with cranberry sauce and chopped fresh mint to
really bring the flavors of Thanksgiving home.*

INGREDIENTS

16 extra-large white button
mushrooms, cleaned

2 tablespoons olive oil, plus extra
for coating mushrooms

Salt (kosher or sea) and
freshly ground black pepper,
to taste

2 medium garlic cloves, minced

1 large shallot, minced

1 stalk celery, diced

¾ pound turkey sausage

1 tablespoon poultry seasoning

1 tablespoon chopped
dried cranberries

1 tablespoon cinnamon applesauce

3 ounces mascarpone cheese,
at room temperature

¼ cup crumbled prepared
corn bread

⅓ cup panko bread crumbs

2 tablespoons plus 2 teaspoons
canna-olive oil

PROCEDURE

1. Prepare the mushrooms as in steps 1–2 on page 63.
2. In a medium skillet, heat the olive oil over medium heat. Add the garlic, shallot, and celery and cook until they are translucent but not browned, 8 to 10 minutes.
3. Add the sausage, poultry seasoning, 1 teaspoon salt, and ½ teaspoon pepper. Cook, breaking the sausage up with a spoon into small pieces, until all the pink has disappeared, about 5 to 7 minutes.
4. Add the cranberries, applesauce, mascarpone, corn bread, and bread crumbs, mixing thoroughly.
5. Remove the skillet from the heat and stir in the cannaoil, mixing thoroughly for 2 minutes.
6. Fill the mushroom caps with 1½ tablespoons each of the sausage mixture.
7. Bake the mushrooms until they are tender and the filling is golden brown on top, about 20 minutes.

MAKES:
16 stuffed mushrooms

SERVING SIZE:
2 mushrooms

DIFFICULTY:
Intermediate

CHICKEN WINGS FIVE WAYS

Chicken wings are another thing we can't get enough of—so we're giving you five different takes on them. Try each variation or all five for your next tailgating party. They are sure to be a hit.

TERIYAKI-STYLE CHICKEN WINGS

These wings are a fun departure from the traditional. The combination of sweet, sour, and salty is a home run.

INGREDIENTS

3 pounds chicken wings, about 24

2 tablespoons vegetable oil

1 teaspoon kosher salt

1 teaspoon freshly ground pepper

¾ cup low-sodium soy sauce

¼ cup orange juice

¼ cup lime juice

1/4 cup hoisin sauce

¼ cup ketchup

¼ cup coconut sugar

3 tablespoons white wine vinegar

½ teaspoon powdered ginger

½ teaspoon garlic powder

2 teaspoons chili powder

2 tablespoons cannaoil

2 tablespoons chopped cashews, for garnish

2 tablespoons chopped fresh cilantro, for garnish

Lime wedges, for serving

PROCEDURE

1. Preheat the oven to 400°F and line 2 baking sheets with parchment paper.
2. Rinse the chicken wings and pat them dry. Cut off wing tips and discard. Separate wings at joint into 2 pieces.
3. Toss wings with vegetable oil to coat and spread out on baking sheets. Sprinkle with salt and pepper.
4. Bake for 15 minutes. Turn wings over and bake an additional 15 minutes until an instant-read thermometer inserted into the wing registers 150°F.
5. While wings are baking, make the sauce. In a medium saucepan over medium-low heat, whisk together the soy sauce, orange juice, lime juice, hoisin sauce, ketchup, coconut sugar, white wine vinegar, ginger, garlic powder, chili powder, and cannaoil.
6. Cook the sauce until it thickens enough to coat the back of a spoon. Remove the pan from the heat.
7. When the wings are cooked, transfer them to a large mixing bowl. Pour the sauce over them and toss the wings with the sauce to coat evenly.
8. Arrange the wings on a serving tray and use a spatula to scrape out any sauce that is left in the bowl, drizzling it over the wings. Garnish with cashews and cilantro and serve with lime wedges.

MAKES:
24 wings (48 pieces)

SERVING SIZE:
4 wings

DIFFICULTY:
Medium

MOROCCAN-STYLE CHICKEN WINGS

Greek yogurt or sour cream makes a quick and easy dipping sauce for these wings. Garam masala is a South Asian spice blend found at most major grocery stores, or use a packaged Moroccan spice blend. If you can't find pomegranate molasses, you can substitute cranberry juice concentrate.

INGREDIENTS

3 pounds chicken wings, about 24

2 tablespoons vegetable oil

3 teaspoons kosher salt, divided

1 teaspoon freshly ground pepper

¾ cup orange juice

¼ cup lemon juice

¼ cup packed brown sugar

¼ cup pomegranate molasses

¼ cup papaya juice

3 tablespoons garam masala
or Moroccan spice blend

Pinch cayenne pepper (optional)

2 tablespoons cannabutter

1 ½ tablespoons chopped fresh
cilantro, for garnish

PROCEDURE

1. Prepare the chicken wings as in steps 1–4 on page 69, using 2 teaspoons of the salt.
2. In a medium saucepan set over medium heat, whisk together the orange juice, lemon juice, brown sugar, pomegranate molasses, papaya juice, garam masala, cayenne, cannabutter, and 1 teaspoon salt.
3. Cook the sauce until it thickens enough to coat the back of a spoon. Remove the pan from the heat.
4. When the wings are cooked, transfer them to a large mixing bowl. Pour the sauce over them and toss the wings with the sauce to coat evenly.
5. Arrange the wings on a serving tray and use a spatula to scrape out any sauce that is left in the bowl, drizzling it over the wings. Garnish with cilantro.

MAKES:
24 wings (48 pieces)

SERVING SIZE:
4 wings

DIFFICULTY:
Medium

TUSCAN-STYLE CHICKEN WINGS

Though lemon, Parmesan, and Italian seasoning might seem like unconventional flavors for wings, trust us—these babies disappear fast at parties.

MAKES:

24 wings (48 pieces)

SERVING SIZE:

4 wings

DIFFICULTY:

Medium

INGREDIENTS

3 pounds chicken wings, about 24

2 tablespoons vegetable oil

2 teaspoons kosher salt

1 teaspoon freshly ground pepper

1 tablespoon freshly grated lemon zest (from 2 medium lemons)

2 tablespoons freshly squeezed lemon juice (from 1 medium lemon)

½ tablespoon honey

2 teaspoons minced garlic

2 teaspoons Italian seasoning blend

1 teaspoon red pepper flakes

1 teaspoon lemon pepper

½ teaspoon sea salt

2 tablespoons cannaoil

2 tablespoons extra-virgin olive oil

¼ cup freshly grated Parmesan cheese, for garnish

1 ½ tablespoons chopped fresh Italian parsley

PROCEDURE

1. Prepare the chicken wings as in steps 1–4 on page 69.
2. In a medium saucepan over medium heat, whisk together the lemon zest and juice, honey, garlic, Italian seasoning, red pepper flakes, lemon pepper, and sea salt. Slowly whisk in the cannaoil and olive oil, mixing thoroughly, 1 to 2 minutes.
3. Cook the sauce until it thickens enough to coat the back of a spoon. Remove the pan from the heat.
4. When the wings are cooked, transfer them to a large mixing bowl. Pour the sauce over them and toss the wings with the sauce to coat evenly.
5. Arrange the wings on a serving tray and use a spatula to scrape out any sauce that is left in the bowl, drizzling it over the wings. Garnish with Parmesan and parsley.

THAI-STYLE CHICKEN WINGS

Think of this as chicken satay in wings form. If you like things spicy, add more sriracha. The easiest way to melt cannabutter is to heat it in the microwave for 10-second intervals, stirring after each one until it's fully liquefied. And, finally, zest your lime before juicing it—if you juice it first, it'll be much harder to remove the zest.

INGREDIENTS

3 pounds chicken wings, about 24

2 tablespoons vegetable oil

2 teaspoons kosher salt

1 teaspoon freshly ground pepper

¼ cup coconut milk

¼ cup Thai peanut sauce

1 tablespoon sriracha

Zest and juice of 1 lime

2 tablespoons cannabutter, melted

¼ cup finely chopped roasted peanuts, for garnish

PROCEDURE

1. Prepare the chicken wings as in steps 1–4 on page 69.
2. In a medium saucepan over medium heat, whisk together the coconut milk, peanut sauce, sriracha, and lime zest and juice. Slowly whisk in the cannabutter, mixing thoroughly, 1 to 2 minutes.
3. Cook the sauce until it thickens enough to coat the back of a spoon. Remove the pan from the heat.
4. When the wings are cooked, transfer them to a large mixing bowl. Pour the sauce over them and toss the wings with the sauce to coat evenly.
5. Arrange the wings on a serving tray and use a spatula to scrape out any sauce that is left in the bowl, drizzling it over the wings. Garnish with peanuts.

MAKES:
24 wings (48 pieces)

SERVING SIZE:
4 wings

DIFFICULTY:
Medium

TRADITIONAL BUFFALO-STYLE CHICKEN WINGS

This is the classic wings recipe (but with a little kick of cannabis). Our favorite hot sauce to use is Frank's RedHot. Serve with carrot and celery sticks and your favorite dipping sauce.

INGREDIENTS

3 pounds chicken wings, about 24

2 tablespoons vegetable oil

2 teaspoons kosher salt

1 teaspoon freshly ground pepper

3 tablespoons unsalted butter

½ cup Frank's or other hot sauce of your choice

1 tablespoon sriracha

2 tablespoons cannabutter

3 tablespoons chopped celery leaves

PROCEDURE

1. Prepare the chicken wings as in steps 1–4 on page 67.
2. In a medium saucepan set over medium heat, whisk together the unsalted butter, hot sauce, sriracha, and cannabutter, stirring until cannabutter is completely melted and evenly distributed throughout. Remove the pan from the heat.
3. When the wings are cooked, transfer them to a large mixing bowl. Pour the sauce over them and toss the wings with the sauce to coat evenly.
4. Arrange the wings on a serving tray and use a spatula to scrape out any sauce that is left in the bowl, drizzling it over the wings. Garnish with celery leaves.

MAKES:
24 wings (48 pieces)

SERVING SIZE:
4 wings

DIFFICULTY:
Medium

SPICED NUTS

Sweet, spicy, and salty, these nuts will call to you day and night. Store them in an airtight container—although they won't last long. And if you can't control yourself, make a second batch with canola oil rather than cannaoil (that's what we do).

MAKES:
2½ cups nuts

SERVING SIZE:
¼ cup nuts

DIFFICULTY:
Easy

INGREDIENTS

1 egg white

1 cup pecans

½ cup almonds

½ cup walnuts

½ cup cashews

3 ⅓ tablespoons cannaoil

2 tablespoons packed brown sugar

1 teaspoon chili powder

½ teaspoon ground allspice

½ teaspoon ground cinnamon

Pinch of cayenne pepper

Pinch of ground ginger

PROCEDURE

1. Preheat the oven to 300°F.
2. In a small bowl, beat the egg white until soft and foamy.
3. Put the remaining ingredients in a large bowl, pour the egg white over them, and combine thoroughly.
4. Spread the nut mixture into a single layer on a rimmed baking sheet.
5. Bake, stirring every 10 minutes, until the nuts darken in color and become very fragrant, 30 to 35 minutes.
6. Put the baking pan on a wire rack to cool. The nuts will crisp as they cool—break up any that stick together.

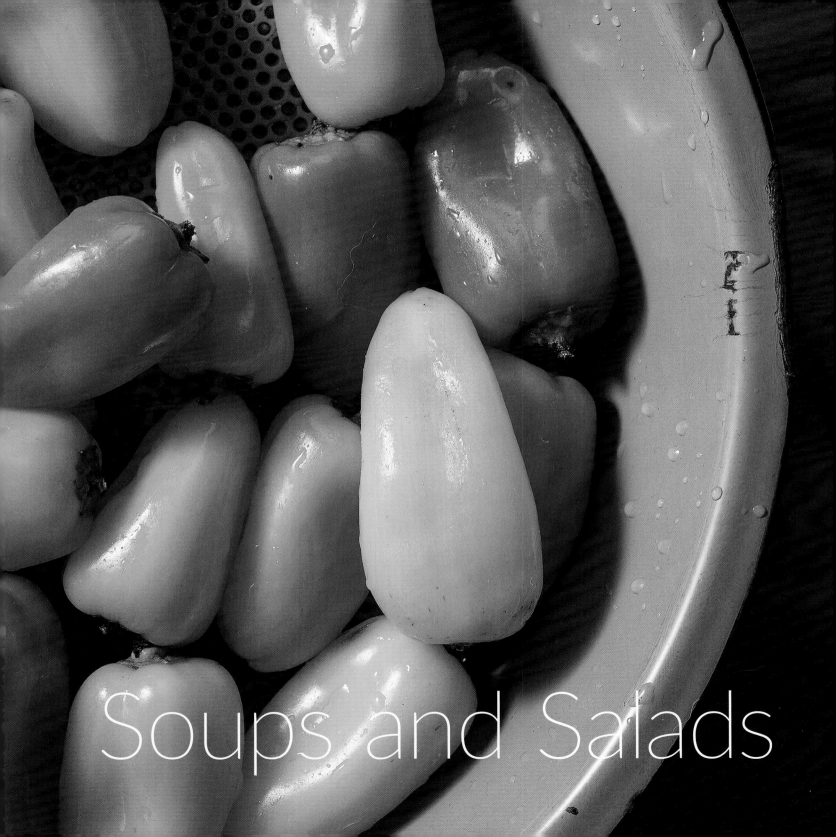

Soups and Salads

BUTTERNUT SQUASH SOUP

Pure flavors and a velvety texture make this soup an HERB favorite. Many markets sell butternut squash already peeled and cut in chunks, which makes the preparation easier and faster. Be sure you let the soup cool before pureeing it, since blending hot liquids can be dangerous and messy.

MAKES:

6 servings

DIFFICULTY:

Intermediate

INGREDIENTS

2 tablespoons cannabutter

1 medium sweet onion, such as Vidalia or Walla Walla, finely diced

1 (2- to 3-pound) butternut squash, peeled, seeded, and cut into 1-inch chunks

5½ cups unsalted chicken stock

½ cup heavy cream

½ teaspoon ground nutmeg

Kosher salt and finely ground fresh black pepper, to taste

PROCEDURE

1. In a large pot, melt the cannabutter over medium-low heat. Add the onions and cook until they are translucent, about 8 minutes.
2. Add the squash and stock. Bring to a simmer and cook until the squash is tender, about 15 to 20 minutes. Stir in the cream, then turn off the heat and let the soup cool slightly.
3. Working in 2 batches, puree the soup in a blender or food processor. Or, if you have an immersion blender, you can puree the soup directly in the pot.
4. Return the blended soup to the pot and rewarm it over medium-low heat. Season with the nutmeg, salt, and pepper before serving.

LENTIL SOUP

Lentil soup always sounds so sad and dull—until we have a bowl and are reminded how warming and rich it can be.

MAKES:

6 servings

DIFFICULTY:

Easy

INGREDIENTS

2 tablespoons canna-olive oil

½ medium onion, diced

1 medium carrot, diced

1 stalk celery, diced

2 garlic cloves, minced

1 quart chicken or vegetable stock

1 (15-ounce) can diced tomatoes

1¼ cups yellow or red lentils, rinsed

1 teaspoon ground cumin

1 teaspoon sherry vinegar

4 strips cooked bacon,
chopped, for garnish

1 cup croutons, for garnish

PROCEDURE

1. In a large pot, heat the canna-olive oil over medium heat. Add the onion, carrot, celery, and garlic and sauté until tender, 7 to 9 minutes.
2. Add the stock, tomatoes, lentils, and cumin, and simmer for 45 minutes.
3. Stir in the vinegar and serve garnished with the bacon and croutons.

CHEFS' NOTES:

For a heartier soup, add cooked sausage, chicken, or even sliced hot dogs.

Use 1 cup less stock to make the dish more stew-like.

Stir in 3 cups fresh baby spinach at the very end of cooking for a pop of color
and an extra shot of vitamins.

TOMATO SOUP

MAKES:

4 servings

DIFFICULTY:

Easy

This is a creamy, warming soup, and the scallion garnish gives it a bright note. Pair a bowl with a Grilled Cheese Sandwich (page 114) for the ultimate soup-sandwich combo.

INGREDIENTS

4 teaspoons canna-olive oil

1 medium onion, chopped

1 quart vegetable or chicken stock

1 (28-ounce) can crushed tomatoes

1 cup half-and-half

Salt (kosher or sea) and freshly ground black pepper, to taste

8 leaves chopped fresh basil or 2 chopped scallions for garnish

4 tablespoons shredded mozzarella

PROCEDURE

1. In a medium pot, heat the cannaoil over medium heat. Add the onions and sauté until translucent, 6 to 7 minutes.
2. Add the stock and tomatoes and cook until they are warmed through. Add the half-and-half and season the soup with salt and pepper. Simmer the soup, stirring occasionally, until it has heated through, 15 to 20 minutes. Turn off the heat and let the soup cool slightly.
3. Working in 2 batches, puree the soup in a blender or food processor. Or, if you have an immersion blender, you can puree the soup directly in the pot.
4. Return the blended soup to the pot and rewarm it over medium-low heat.
5. Garnish with the basil or scallions and mozzarella before serving.

CREAM OF ASPARAGUS SOUP WITH FRIZZLED LEEKS

When asparagus season comes around, our families start requesting this sublime soup. This infused version is strictly adults only, though. Be sure to rinse the leeks very well—their tight layers can hold a surprising amount of dirt.

INGREDIENTS

1¼ pounds asparagus, rinsed, tough stems removed, cut into 1-inch pieces

3 cups vegetable or chicken stock

2 tablespoons butter

4 teaspoons cannabutter

1 garlic clove, chopped

1½ cups thinly sliced leeks, divided

½ cup half-and-half

½ cup canola oil

1 tablespoon freshly grated lemon zest

Salt (kosher or sea) and white pepper, to taste

PROCEDURE

1. In a medium pot, combine the asparagus and stock. Simmer, covered, over medium heat, until the asparagus is tender, about 20 minutes. Reduce the heat to low.
2. In medium skillet, heat the butter and cannabutter over medium-low heat. Add the garlic and 1 cup of the leeks and sauté until the leeks are tender, about 7 to 9 minutes.
3. Add the leek mixture to the soup along with the half-and-half, and cook over low heat 5 minutes. (Do not wash the skillet.) Turn off the heat and let the soup cool slightly.
4. Return the skillet to medium heat and add the oil. When the oil is hot, add the remaining ½ cup leeks and cook until golden brown and crisp, 2 to 3 minutes. Using a slotted spoon, remove the leeks to a clean dish towel or paper towel to drain.
5. Puree the soup in a blender or food processor. Or, if you have an immersion blender, you can puree the soup directly in the pot.
6. Return the blended soup to the pot and rewarm it over medium-low heat.
7. Garnish the soup with the lemon zest and frizzled leeks and season with salt and pepper before serving.

CHEFS' NOTES

This soup is also delicious served chilled.

You can use frozen, thawed asparagus if fresh is not in season. Or substitute fennel or cauliflower for the asparagus—just make sure the vegetables are tender before pureeing the soup.

To make the soup vegan, use vegetable stock and canna-coconut oil instead of cannabutter, and omit the half-and-half (or use a vegan substitute).

CREAMY BROCCOLI AND CHEESE SOUP

We used to avoid broccoli, but this soup changed all that: with a fabulous velvety texture, it hits the spot on a cold day.

INGREDIENTS

2 tablespoons butter

2 tablespoons cannabutter

1 small onion, chopped

3 tablespoons all-purpose flour

2 cups vegetable stock

1 large head broccoli, cut into florets

2 cups milk

1 cup half-and-half

3 cups freshly shredded cheddar cheese, plus extra for garnish

Salt (kosher or sea) and freshly ground black pepper, to taste

PROCEDURE

1. In a large pot, melt the butter and cannabutter over medium-low heat.
2. Add the onion and sauté until translucent, 4 to 5 minutes.
3. Sprinkle in the flour and cook, stirring, for 1 to 2 minutes to eliminate the raw-flour taste, not letting it brown.
4. Add the stock and broccoli and cook for 9 minutes. Turn off the heat and let the soup cool slightly.
5. Working in 2 batches, puree the soup in a blender or food processor. Or, if you have an immersion blender, you can puree the soup directly in the pot.
6. Return the blended soup to the pot. Over medium-low heat, add the milk, half-and-half, and cheddar, and stir until cheese melts.
7. Season the soup with salt and pepper, and garnish with more cheddar before serving.

WHITE BEAN SOUP WITH KIELBASA AND KALE

MAKES:

6 servings

DIFFICULTY:

Easy

Melissa came up with this take on the classic Italian soup. It's a hearty, soulful recipe that pairs meaty kielbasa sausage with earthy kale and filling white beans, a winning combination.

INGREDIENTS

1 pound dried white beans, such as navy or great northern

2 tablespoons canna-olive oil

1 cup sliced or cubed kielbasa

1 cup packed shredded lacinato kale leaves, stems discarded

2 medium onions, chopped

4 garlic cloves, minced

1 carrot, chopped

2 teaspoons chopped fresh rosemary

6 cups chicken stock

4 cups water

Salt (kosher or sea) and freshly ground black pepper, to taste

PROCEDURE

1. Put the beans in a large pot and cover them with water by 2 inches. Bring the water to a boil, then turn off the heat. Let the beans sit for 1 hour.
2. After an hour, drain the water, rinse the beans, and set them aside in a large bowl. Clean out the pot.
3. In the pot, heat the canna-olive oil over medium heat. Cook the kielbasa, stirring occasionally, until it is slightly browned, 5 to 7 minutes.
4. Stir in the kale and onions and sauté until tender, 7 to 9 minutes.
5. Add the garlic, carrot, and rosemary. Mix well.
6. Add the beans along with the stock and water. Season the soup with salt and pepper.
7. Cook the soup for 45 to 55 minutes, stirring occasionally. If it gets too thick, add water ¼ cup at a time. The soup is done when the beans are soft and mostly broken up.

CHEFS' NOTE

If you like a creamier soup, pull out some of the beans before adding them with the stock in step 6, puree them, and add them back to the pot before serving.

LIME CURRY CHICKPEA SALAD

This one-bowl dish is easy to make, and it's also good for you. It's filling enough to be a meal on its own, or it makes a terrific side. You can find Aleppo pepper online and at gourmet or major grocery stores, but a good substitute is 4 parts sweet paprika to 1 part cayenne pepper.

MAKES:

4 servings

DIFFICULTY:

Easy

INGREDIENTS

2 tablespoons cider vinegar

2 tablespoons extra-virgin olive oil

4 teaspoons canna-olive oil

1 tablespoon honey

1 tablespoon freshly squeezed lime juice

2 teaspoons curry powder

1 teaspoon salt (kosher or sea)

1 teaspoon ground cumin

½ teaspoon ground turmeric

½ teaspoon Aleppo pepper

2 (15-ounce) cans chickpeas, rinsed and drained

½ medium bell pepper, any color, seeded and chopped

½ medium red onion, chopped

½ cup chopped fresh parsley

Pita chips, for serving

PROCEDURE

In a large bowl, thoroughly combine all the ingredients except the pita chips. Let the salad sit at room temperature for 30 minutes before serving, for the flavors to combine.

CHEFS' NOTES

For a delicious vegetarian sandwich, serve the salad in pita pockets.

For variety and substance, add chopped chicken, shrimp, or tofu, and ripe avocado.

SPICY TOFU AND CASHEW SALAD WITH KIMCHI VINAIGRETTE

MAKES:

6 servings

SERVING SIZE:

⅙ salad and
2 teaspoons dressing

DIFFICULTY:

Intermediate

We were late converts to tofu but have come to appreciate how well it absorbs flavorings. This dish pairs soba noodles, cubes of tofu, and crunchy vegetables and nuts with a spicy vinaigrette. Fish sauce can be found online, at Asian markets, and, increasingly, at major grocery stores.

INGREDIENTS

For the vinaigrette:
1 tablespoon store-bought kimchi

2 tablespoons liquid from
the kimchi

1 teaspoon fish sauce (*nam pla*)

2 tablespoons cannaoil

For the soba noodles:
1 (8-ounce) package soba noodles

Vegetable oil, for coating
the noodles

For the tofu:
1 (14-ounce) package
extra-firm tofu

1 teaspoon garlic salt

½ teaspoon cayenne pepper

¼ teaspoon red pepper flakes

Freshly ground black pepper,
to taste

½ teaspoon vegetable oil

For the salad:
1 cup julienned sugar snap peas

1 large carrot, diced

½ cup chopped cashews, toasted

½ cup chopped fresh cilantro leaves

PROCEDURE

Make the vinaigrette:

1. In the bowl of a food processor fitted with a metal blade, pulse the kimchi, kimchi liquid, and fish sauce until the mixture becomes a smooth paste. With the machine running, add the cannaoil in a steady stream through the feed tube. Blend for 1 minute to incorporate the oil. Set the dressing aside.

Make the soba noodles:

2. Cook the noodles according to package directions. Drain them and, in a medium bowl, toss them in a drizzle of vegetable oil. Spread them in an even layer on a baking sheet to cool.

Make the tofu:

3. Drain the tofu thoroughly, wrap it in paper towels, and pat it dry, squeezing out any excess moisture. Chop the tofu into 1-inch cubes and put them in a large glass bowl.

4. Add the garlic salt, cayenne, red pepper flakes, black pepper, and vegetable oil, and rub them into the tofu to distribute the spices evenly.

Make the salad:

5. Add the snap peas, carrots, and noodles to the bowl with the tofu. Pour the dressing over the salad and toss well to combine.

6. Top with the cashews and cilantro before serving.

ASIAN CHICKEN SALAD WITH WASABI VINAIGRETTE

Laurie recently went to a potluck dinner—with emphasis on the "pot." She brought three cannasalads, and this one was the most popular. Everyone wanted the recipe—so here it is.

MAKES:

4 servings

SERVING SIZE:

¼ salad and
2 teaspoons dressing

DIFFICULTY:

Easy

INGREDIENTS

For the dressing:
Zest and juice of 1 lime

2 tablespoons prepared wasabi

2 tablespoons seasoned
rice wine vinegar

4 teaspoons cannaoil

1 tablespoon peanut oil

1 tablespoon low-sodium soy sauce

1 teaspoon agave nectar or honey

¼ teaspoon ground ginger

Freshly ground black pepper,
to taste

For the salad:
2½ cups shredded cooked chicken
(from 8 ounces chicken breast)

½ head napa cabbage, shredded

½ head romaine lettuce, chopped

2 large carrots, shredded

2 stalks celery, thinly sliced

4 green onions (white and green
parts), cut on a diagonal

1 cup julienned snow peas

½ cup chopped fresh mint leaves

½ cup chopped fresh cilantro leaves

½ cup chopped roasted
unsalted peanuts

PROCEDURE

Make the dressing:
1. Put all the ingredients in a glass jar with a tight-fitting lid. Screw the lid on, making sure the seal is tight, and shake vigorously to combine.

Make the salad:
2. Combine all the ingredients except the peanuts in a large glass bowl. Pour the dressing over the salad and toss well to combine.
3. Top with the peanuts before serving.

THAI SHRIMP SALAD

This is a great warm-weather salad, with an interesting mix of flavors, colors, and textures. We love pairing shrimp with papaya, and the garnishes of mint, cilantro, and peanuts really bring it all together. If you don't have coconut palm sugar, brown sugar will work fine.

MAKES:

4 servings

SERVING SIZE:

¼ salad and
2 teaspoons dressing

DIFFICULTY:

Easy

INGREDIENTS

½ cup freshly squeezed lime juice
(from about 4 medium lines)

2 tablespoons Thai fish sauce
(*nam pla*)

4 teaspoons cannaoil

2 teaspoons coconut palm sugar

1 small onion, chopped

1 serrano chile, seeded and chopped

2 garlic cloves, minced

1 pound medium or large shrimp,
peeled, deveined, and cooked

2 medium green papayas,
sliced or cubed

2 carrots, shredded

8 leaves fresh mint, for garnish

¼ cup cilantro, for garnish

¼ cup peanuts, for garnish

PROCEDURE

1. In a medium bowl, whisk together the lime juice, fish sauce, cannaoil, sugar, onion, chile, and garlic.
2. In a large serving bowl, combine the shrimp, papayas, and carrots. Pour the dressing over the salad and toss well to combine.
3. Garnish with the mint, cilantro, and peanuts before serving.

Sandwiches

CHICKEN BANH MI

The banh mi is a Vietnamese sandwich. It can be made with a variety of fillings and condiments; our version has sliced chicken, shredded cabbage and carrots, and a salty, garlicky, citrusy dressing. Use the best bread you can find—we recommend a light, airy French baguette with a thin crust. Serve the banh mi immediately; otherwise, the bread can get soggy.

MAKES:

2 sandwiches

SERVING SIZE:

1 sandwich

DIFFICULTY:

Easy

INGREDIENTS

2 tablespoons water

1 tablespoon freshly squeezed lime juice

2 teaspoons Thai fish sauce (*nam pla*)

2 teaspoons cannaoil

1 teaspoon toasted sesame oil

1 small garlic clove, minced

1 teaspoon soy sauce

1 tablespoon sugar

2 6-inch-long slices baguette, split in half lengthwise

2 rotisserie chicken breasts, thinly sliced

¼ cup shredded napa cabbage

¼ cup shredded carrots

6 cilantro sprigs

PROCEDURE

1. In a small bowl, whisk together the water, lime juice, fish sauce, cannaoil, sesame oil, garlic, soy sauce, and sugar until the sugar is dissolved and the dressing is well combined.
2. Drizzle the dressing over the cut sides of the bread. Arrange the sliced chicken on the sandwich and top with the shredded vegetables and cilantro sprigs. Use a spatula to spoon any sauce remaining in the bowl on top.

CHEFS' NOTES

Cooked, sliced pork (tenderloin, shoulder, or butt) makes a great substitute for the chicken.

For a vegetarian version, omit the fish sauce and chicken, and marinate cubes of extra-firm tofu in the sauce/dressing.

BLATS (BACON, LETTUCE, AVOCADO, AND TOMATO)

MAKES:

2 sandwiches

SERVING SIZE:

1 sandwich

DIFFICULTY:

Easy

What could be better than a BLT, you might ask? A BLAT! This recipe deserves the best ingredients you can afford: good-quality bacon, a ripe avocado, homemade mayo, and a perfect tomato make a truly remarkable sandwich.

INGREDIENTS

½ firm-ripe avocado, peeled, pitted, and thinly sliced

2 teaspoons freshly squeezed lemon juice

4 slices potato bread

4 tablespoons Canna-Mayonnaise (recipe below)

8 strips bacon, cooked as you like it and drained

4 leaves soft lettuce, such as Boston, rinsed and patted dry

4 slices ripe tomato

PROCEDURE

1. In a small bowl, toss the avocado gently in the lemon juice, keeping the slices intact. Set the avocado aside.
2. Toast the bread.
3. While the bread is still warm, spread 1 tablespoon canna-mayonnaise on each slice.
4. Layer 2 bacon strips, 2 lettuce leaves, a few avocado slices, and 2 tomato slices on a bread slice, top with another bread slice, and repeat for the other sandwich.
5. Cut each sandwich in half before serving.

CANNA-MAYONNAISE

Canna-mayonnaise will keep, refrigerated, for five days.

INGREDIENTS

1 large egg

1 tablespoon Dijon mustard

1 cup canola oil

1⅓ tablespoons cannaoil

4 teaspoons white wine vinegar or freshly squeezed lemon juice

Salt (kosher or sea) and freshly ground black pepper, to taste

PROCEDURE

1. In the bowl of a food processor fitted with the metal blade, pulse the egg and mustard until evenly combined.
2. With the machine running, add the canola and cannaoil in a steady stream through the feed tube. Add the vinegar and pulse until smooth. Season with salt and pepper.

MAKES:

1¼ cups mayonnaise

SERVING SIZE:

2 tablespoons mayonnaise

DIFFICULTY:

Easy

TURKEY, HAVARTI, AND CARAMELIZED ONION SANDWICHES

Mild turkey and Havarti meld perfectly with the sweetness of roasted red pepper and the layered flavors of Melissa's genius caramelized onion dip.

MAKES:
2 sandwiches

SERVING SIZE:
1 Sandwich

DIFFICULTY:
Easy

INGREDIENTS

2 ciabatta rolls, cut in half lengthwise

½ cup Caramelized Onion Dip (page 41)

4 strips jarred roasted red pepper

6 slices Havarti cheese

8 slices roast or smoked turkey

PROCEDURE

1. Toast the rolls.
2. Spread each roll on both sides with the onion dip.
3. Layer 2 pepper strips, 3 Havarti slices, and 4 turkey slices on the bottom of each roll, then top the roll.
4. Slice each sandwich in half before serving.

CHEFS' NOTE
Adding a few strips of bacon would make this great sandwich even better.

MEDITERRANEAN VEGGIE AND HUMMUS SANDWICHES

MAKES:
2 sandwiches

SERVING SIZE:
1 sandwich

DIFFICULTY:
Easy

This healthy hummus sandwich (in its nonmedicated form) has come to work with Laurie on many occasions. She's the envy of those who have something far less delicious in their brown paper bags.

INGREDIENTS

3 tablespoons olive oil

1 small zucchini, cut into thin strips

1 bell pepper, any color, seeded and cut into thin strips

1 small red onion, thinly sliced

1 teaspoon ground cumin

½ teaspoon dried oregano

Salt (kosher or sea) and freshly ground pepper, to taste

½ cup Hummus (page 42)

4 slices whole-grain bread

PROCEDURE

1. Preheat the oven to 375°F.
2. Pour the olive oil onto a rimmed baking sheet. Put the zucchini, bell pepper, and onion slices on the baking sheet and sprinkle with the cumin, oregano, salt, and pepper. Toss to coat and bake until the vegetables are tender, 15 to 20 minutes. Let the veggies cool.
3. Spread the hummus equally on all four slices of bread.
4. Divide the vegetables between 2 bread slices, add more salt and pepper to taste, and top with the remaining 2 slices of bread,
5. Slice each sandwich in half before serving.

CHEFS' NOTE

Try this sandwich as a wrap instead, with spinach tortillas in place of the bread.

CUBANOS

We think the Cubano is one of the best sandwiches in the world. The combination of pickles, pork, sauce, and melty cheese, all encased in a warm roll, can't be beat.

MAKES:
2 sandwiches

SERVING SIZE:
1 sandwich

DIFFICULTY:
Easy

INGREDIENTS

2 (8-inch) Cuban-style rolls (or soft rolls), cut in half lengthwise

¼ cup mayonnaise

2 teaspoons canna-canola oil

2 tablespoons yellow mustard

6 slices roast pork

6 slices Swiss cheese

6 slices ham

16 dill pickle chips

PROCEDURE

1. Spread the mayo on the bottom half of the rolls and spread the tops with the canna-canola oil and mustard.
2. Layer 3 slices of roast pork, 3 slices Swiss, 3 ham slices, and 8 pickle chips on the bottom of each roll, then top the roll.
3. Heat a nonstick skillet over medium-low heat.
4. Cook the sandwiches, pressing down frequently with a spatula, until the rolls are golden brown and the cheese is melted, 7 to 9 minutes.

GRILLED CHEESE SANDWICHES

We like this all-American classic with a combination of cheddar and Gruyère cheeses.

MAKES:

4 sandwiches

SERVING SIZE:

1 sandwich

DIFFICULTY:

Easy

INGREDIENTS

1 tablespoon unsalted butter, softened

2 teaspoons cannabutter, softened

2 teaspoons Dijon mustard

8 slices crusty bread

4 slices cheddar

4 slices Gruyère cheese

1 tablespoon olive oil

PROCEDURE

1. In a small bowl, combine the butter, cannabutter, and Dijon. Spread the mixture on all 8 slices of the bread.
2. Layer 1 slice of cheddar and 1 of Gruyère on the unbuttered side of 4 of the slices.
3. In a large nonstick skillet, heat the olive oil over medium heat.
4. Cook all 8 slices until the bread is golden brown and the cheese melts.
5. Pair top and bottom halves to make sandwiches, cut in half, and serve warm.

PHILLY CHEESESTEAKS

Our Cheddar Cheese Sauce subs for the usual provolone in this tasty sandwich.

MAKES:

2 sandwiches

SERVING SIZE:

1 sandwich

DIFFICULTY:

Medium

INGREDIENTS

2 tablespoons olive oil

1 bell pepper, any color, thinly sliced

½ medium red onion, thinly sliced

6 slices roast beef

2 hero or hoagie rolls, cut in half lengthwise

½ cup Cheddar Cheese Sauce (page 49)

PROCEDURE

1. In a large sauté pan, heat the olive oil over medium heat.
2. Add the bell pepper and cook until softened, 8 to 10 minutes.
3. Add the onion and cook until soft and translucent, 6 to 7 minutes more. Set the vegetables aside.
4. In the same pan, sauté the roast beef, adding a little more olive oil if the pan is dry.
5. Return the vegetables to the pan to heat through.
6. Divide the roast beef mixture between the bottoms of the rolls.
7. Pour the cheese sauce over the mixture, top the rolls, and serve immediately.

Pizza, Pastas, and Risotto

GARDEN PIZZA

This is our take on the salad pizza, which combines two delicious things (you got it—salad and pizza) into one easy-to-eat meal.

MAKES:

1 8-inch pizza

SERVING SIZE:

½ pizza

DIFFICULTY:

Easy

INGREDIENTS

1 small (8-inch) store-bought pizza crust, such as Boboli

2 tablespoons extra-virgin olive oil, divided

2 cups salad greens

¼ cup chopped bell peppers, any color

¼ cup chopped red onion

2 tablespoons balsamic vinegar

Kosher salt and coarsely ground fresh black pepper, to taste

2 teaspoons cannaoil

¼ cup goat cheese (optional)

PROCEDURE

1. Preheat the oven to 400°F.
2. Put the crust on a baking sheet and drizzle it with 1 tablespoon of the olive oil. Bake according to package directions.
3. Put the salad greens, peppers, and onion in a medium bowl. In a small bowl, combine the vinegar, salt, and pepper, and whisk in the remaining tablespoon of olive oil and the cannaoil.
4. Pour the vinaigrette over the greens and toss to combine.
5. Top the crust with the dressed greens and goat cheese, if using.

PIZZA BIANCA WITH MUSHROOMS, FONTINA, AND ROSEMARY

A pizza bianca ("white pizza") is simply a pizza made without tomato sauce. Fontina cheese has an earthy taste that pairs perfectly with the mushrooms and rosemary here.

MAKES:

1 8-inch pizza

SERVING SIZE:

½ pizza

DIFFICULTY:

Easy

INGREDIENTS

1 small (8-inch) store-bought pizza crust, such as Boboli

2 teaspoons extra-virgin olive oil

½ cup Béchamel Sauce (recipe page 125), at room temperature

3 cremini mushrooms, wiped clean and sliced

1 tablespoon chopped fresh rosemary

Generous pinch of red pepper flakes

¼ cup freshly shredded fontina cheese, at room temperature

PROCEDURE

1. Preheat the oven to 400°F.
2. Put the crust on a baking sheet and drizzle it with the olive oil. Bake according to package directions, but remove the crust 5 minutes before the time suggested.
3. Reduce the oven temperature to 340°F. Spread the béchamel over the crust. Top with the mushrooms, rosemary, red pepper flakes, and fontina.
4. Bake the pizza until the cheese melts, 4 to 5 minutes.

BÉCHAMEL SAUCE

In addition to being a great topper for a white pizza, béchamel sauce is also an essential ingredient in lasagna, vegetable gratin, and macaroni and cheese. It's a good recipe to have in your back pocket.

MAKES:

2½ cups

SERVING SIZE:

¼ cup

DIFFICULTY:

Intermediate

INGREDIENTS

3 tablespoons cannabutter

¼ cup all-purpose flour

Pinch of salt (kosher or sea)

Pinch of white pepper

2 cups warm milk

PROCEDURE

1. In a small saucepan, melt the cannabutter over low heat.
2. Whisk in the flour, salt, and pepper until smooth.
3. Slowly add the milk, whisking to prevent lumps. Simmer the sauce until it is thick enough to coat the back of a spoon, 5 to 7 minutes.

SOPPRESSATA AND GREEN ONION PIZZA

MAKES:
1 8-inch pizza

SERVING SIZE:
¼ pizza

DIFFICULTY:
Easy

Soppressata is a dry Italian salami, similar to pepperoni. It's been showing up recently in restaurants across the country as a pizza topping. After trying it, we decided that we prefer it to pepperoni, so we're using it here for a new take on an old favorite. Soppressatas can range from mild to quite spicy, so choose one that suits your taste.

INGREDIENTS

1 small (8-inch) store-bought
pizza crust, such as Boboli

2 tablespoons extra-virgin olive oil

1 cup Tomato Sauce (recipe below),
at room temperature

1½ cups mozzarella (shredded)
or 6 ounces (sliced), at room
temperature

4 ounces thinly sliced soppressata

¼ cup chopped green onions

Coarsely ground fresh black
pepper, to taste

PROCEDURE

1. Preheat the oven to 400°F.
2. Put the crust on a baking sheet and drizzle it with the olive oil. Bake according to package directions, but remove the crust 5 minutes before the time suggested.
3. Reduce the oven temperature to 340°F.
4. Spread the tomato sauce over the crust. Top with the mozzarella, soppressata, green onions, and pepper.
5. Bake the pizza until the cheese melts, 6 to 8 minutes.

TOMATO SAUCE

We think having a good red sauce recipe is a must—plus, it makes your house smell great while it's cooking. Extra sauce may be frozen up to three months.

INGREDIENTS

⅓ cup canna-olive oil

½ large red onion, minced

2 cloves garlic, minced

1 (15-ounce) can whole peeled
San Marzano tomatoes with juice

1 (6-ounce) can tomato paste

1 (15-ounce) can crushed tomatoes

5 fresh basil leaves

2 tablespoons sugar

1 teaspoon red pepper flakes

½ teaspoon dried oregano

½ teaspoon freshly ground
black pepper

½ teaspoon kosher salt

PROCEDURE

1. In a large saucepan, heat the cannaoil over medium-low heat. Add the onion and garlic and cook, stirring often, until the onions are translucent.
2. Pour the whole tomatoes with the juice into a large glass bowl and crush them with a potato masher or by hand.
3. Add the tomatoes and tomato paste to the pan and stir until smooth. Cook 3 more minutes.
4. Stir in the remaining ingredients (except the fresh basil, if using), mixing well. Cover the pan with a tight-fitting lid and simmer the sauce for 25 minutes. If you're using the fresh basil, tear the leaves into small pieces and stir them into the sauce. Taste the sauce and adjust the seasonings.
5. Simmer for another 5 minutes and serve.

MAKES:
4 cups

SERVING SIZE:
¼ cup

DIFFICULTY:
Intermediate

BAKED PASTA WITH ARTICHOKE PESTO

MAKES:

4 servings

DIFFICULTY:

Easy

Laurie's mother used to make a baked pasta using canned soup. That dish inspired this updated, more sophisticated version—think of it as pasta meets artichoke dip.

INGREDIENTS

1¼ cups artichoke hearts, canned, jarred, or frozen (thawed and drained if frozen)

1 cup packed fresh parsley leaves plus 2 tablespoons chopped parsley

½ cup walnuts

Zest and juice of 1 lemon

3 garlic cloves, minced

½ teaspoon salt (kosher or sea)

⅛ teaspoon freshly ground black pepper

½ cup extra-virgin olive oil

4 teaspoons canna-olive oil

1 pound orecchiette, orzo, or small elbows, cooked al dente

½ cup freshly grated Parmesan cheese

½ cup panko bread crumbs

PROCEDURE

1. Preheat the oven to 340°F.
2. In the bowl of a food processor fitted with the metal blade, pulse the artichoke hearts, 1 cup of the parsley, walnuts, lemon zest and juice, garlic, salt, and pepper until smooth. With the machine running, add the olive oil and canna-olive oil in a steady stream through the feed tube to make a pesto.
3. In a large bowl, combine the pesto with the cooked pasta.
4. Transfer the pasta to a medium (1 quart) casserole dish or 4 individual (1 cup) ramekins, filling it to the top.
5. In a small bowl, combine the Parmesan, bread crumbs, and chopped parsley and sprinkle the mixture evenly on top of the pasta. Bake until the cheese and bread crumbs are golden brown, 20 to 25 minutes.

CHEFS' NOTE

Stir in chicken or bacon, or raw baby spinach, before baking.

SPAGHETTI WITH ARUGULA PESTO

This pasta has a double hit of arugula—it's blended into the tangy and earthy pesto, and then raw leaves are tossed with the finished pasta. We love this pesto and always keep some on hand to spread on sandwiches and bruschetta.

MAKES:
4 servings

DIFFICULTY:
Easy

INGREDIENTS

6 cups packed arugula plus 1 bunch baby arugula

½ cup walnuts

4 garlic cloves, peeled

½ teaspoon salt (kosher or sea)

¼ teaspoon freshly ground black pepper

½ cup plus 2 tablespoons extra-virgin olive oil, divided

4 teaspoons canna-olive oil

¼ cup freshly grated Parmesan cheese, plus more for serving

1 pound spaghetti

PROCEDURE

1. Bring a large pot of salted water to a boil for the spaghetti.
2. In the bowl of a food processor fitted with the metal blade, pulse 6 cups of the arugula, walnuts, garlic, salt, and pepper until pureed. With the machine running, add the ½ cup olive oil and canna-olive oil in a steady stream through the feed tube to make a pesto. Stir in the Parmesan and set the pesto aside.
3. Cook the spaghetti according to package directions.
4. Drain the spaghetti, return it to the pot off the heat, and toss it with the pesto and baby arugula.
5. Divide the pasta among 4 plates, drizzle with the remaining 2 tablespoons olive oil, and top with extra Parmesan.

CHEFS' NOTES

This dish would also be wonderful with the addition of cooked shrimp, scallops, or chicken.

If you don't like arugula, or prefer a milder flavor, substitute baby spinach.

OLD-FASHIONED MACARONI AND CHEESE

SERVES:

8

DIFFICULTY:

Intermediate

Everyone's favorite childhood dish, macaroni and cheese still tops the list of comfort foods we crave. Our take on it has a crunchy bread-crumb crust that provides an irresistible textural contrast to the gooey, cheesy pasta beneath.

INGREDIENTS

8 ounces small elbow macaroni (about 2 cups)

1 teaspoon vegetable oil

¼ cup (½ stick) butter

8 teaspoons cannabutter

1 tablespoon all-purpose flour

1 cup milk

1 cup half-and-half

½ teaspoon salt (kosher or sea)

Pinch of freshly ground pepper

2¼ cups good-quality medium-sharp freshly shredded cheddar cheese, divided

½ cup cheddar crackers, such as Cheez-Its, crushed

½ cup panko bread crumbs

PROCEDURE

1. Preheat the oven to 340°F and bring a large pot of salted water to a boil for the macaroni.
2. Cook the macaroni al dente, according to package directions.
3. Drain the macaroni and rinse it with cold water. Return it to the pot off the heat, toss it with the vegetable oil, and set it aside.
4. In a large saucepan, melt the butter and cannabutter over medium-low heat. Whisk in the flour, then whisk in the milk, half-and-half, salt, and pepper. Cook, stirring, until the mixture thickens enough to coat the back of a spoon, 3 to 4 minutes.
5. Stir in 2 cups of the cheddar and mix well.
6. Add the cooled pasta to the cheese mixture, mixing thoroughly.
7. Turn the mixture into a buttered 9-by-13-inch casserole dish.
8. In a small bowl, combine the remaining ¼ cup cheddar, cheddar crackers, and panko and sprinkle the mixture evenly on top of the pasta.
9. Bake until the topping is golden brown, 30 to 40 minutes.

WILD MUSHROOM PAPPARDELLE WITH PEAS & GOAT CHEESE

MAKES:

4 servings

DIFFICULTY:

Intermediate

This pasta dish combines creamy goat cheese with wild mushrooms for an easy entrée that's fancy enough for company. Pappardelle is a wide-ribbon pasta available in most major groceries.

INGREDIENTS

14 ounces wild mushrooms, such as chanterelles, morels, maitakes, or whatever is available/seasonal

¼ cup extra-virgin olive oil

2 shallots, minced

1 garlic clove, minced

4 ounces goat cheese, at room temperature, plus more for serving

½ cup vegetable stock

Sea salt and freshly ground pepper, to taste

1 pound pappardelle

1 (10-ounce) package frozen peas, thawed and drained

3 tablespoons freshly grated Parmesan cheese

Zest and juice of ½ lemon

4 teaspoons Rémoulade Cannabutter (page 31)

¼ cup chopped Italian parsley, for garnish

PROCEDURE

1. Rub the mushrooms gently with a damp paper towel to remove any dirt (do not run them under water—they will get soggy), and coarsely chop them.
2. Bring a large pot of liberally salted water to a boil for the pasta.
3. In a large skillet, heat the olive oil over medium heat. Add the shallots and sauté until they begin to turn light golden brown, about 2 to 3 minutes. Add the garlic and mushrooms. Sauté until mushrooms have softened, and released most of their liquid, about 5 to 7 minutes.
4. Stir in the goat cheese.
5. Add the vegetable stock and reduce the heat to low. Simmer the mushrooms for 3 minutes, until most of the liquid has been absorbed, then season with salt and pepper.
6. Cook the pappardelle according to package directions. Reserve ½ cup of the water before draining the pasta, and set it aside.
7. Add the drained pasta to the skillet with the mushrooms.
8. Stir in the peas, Parmesan, lemon zest and juice, and cannabutter, and keep stirring for 2 minutes until the sauce is thick enough to just coat the back of a spoon. (If needed, add the reserved pasta water, 1 tablespoon at a time, to bring the sauce to the desired consistency.)
9. Just before serving, top with the parsley and extra goat cheese.

BBQ PORK SPAGHETTI WITH DILL PICKLE PICO DE GALLO

This dish takes comfort food to a whole new level, with a fresh take on pico de gallo to add a bright note. If you have cooked pork on hand, you can skip the roasting, making this an easy dish to put together on a weekday. We like to use a tangy, thick Kansas City–style sauce that really clings to the pasta, but feel free to substitute your favorite barbecue sauce.

INGREDIENTS

For the pico de gallo:
Juice of ½ lime

1 tablespoon cider vinegar

½ teaspoon honey

½ teaspoon sea salt

1 teaspoon freshly ground black pepper

½ cup chopped dill pickle chips, patted dry with paper towels

½ large white onion, finely diced

¼ cup chopped fresh Italian parsley

⅛ cup chopped fresh cilantro

For the tenderloin:
¾ pound pork tenderloin (fat trimmed), at room temperature

1 tablespoon garlic salt

Freshly ground black pepper

2 tablespoons vegetable oil, divided

1 poblano chile, stemmed, seeded, and cut into thin strips

1/2 large white onion, finely diced

1 garlic clove, minced

¼ cup low-sodium beef stock

3½ cups your favorite barbecue sauce

For the spaghetti:
¾ pound spaghetti

4 teaspoons canna-vegetable oil

PROCEDURE

Make the pico de gallo:

1. In a large bowl, whisk together the lime juice, vinegar, honey, salt, and pepper. Add the pickles, onions, parsley, and cilantro, and toss to combine. Cover and refrigerate until needed.

Make the pork:

2. Preheat the oven to 425°F and have a baking sheet handy.

3. Pat the tenderloin dry, and season it liberally with garlic salt and black pepper.

4. In an extra-large skillet or Dutch oven with a tight-fitting lid, heat 1 tablespoon of the vegetable oil over medium-high heat, swirling it to coat the bottom of the pan. When the oil is hot (it will ripple and a drop of water sprinkled in the pan will sizzle), sear the tenderloin on all sides, until it is golden brown, about 3 minutes per side.

5. Transfer the tenderloin to the baking sheet. Roast until an instant-read thermometer inserted into the center of the tenderloin registers 145°F, 15 to 20 minutes. Remove the pork from the oven and let it rest, tented with aluminum foil, at room temperature for 15 minutes.

6. Once pork is done resting, use 2 forks to shred meat, cover with foil, and set aside.

7. Bring a large pot of liberally salted water to a boil for the spaghetti. Cook spaghetti according to package direction.

8. While pasta is cooking, discard any juices or fat from the skillet or Dutch oven the meat was seared in. Set it over medium heat and add the remaining tablespoon of vegetable oil.

9. Add the chile and onion and sauté until the vegetables are a light golden brown, about 5 minutes. Reduce the heat to low.

10. Add the shredded tenderloin to the skillet or Dutch oven along with garlic, beef stock, barbecue sauce, and a healthy dose of pepper. Combine all ingredients and allow to heat through.

11. When the spaghetti is cooked, drain and add to the tenderloin mixture. Stir in the cannaoil, and toss all ingredients to combine.

12. Transfer the BBQ pork spaghetti to a serving dish and top with the pico de gallo.

AVOCADO CRAB PASTA

Though you might think of avocado mostly as a tasty sandwich addition or guacamole ingredient, in this recipe it teams up with herbs and citrus to make a wonderfully creamy uncooked sauce for pasta. This is a quick dish if you get your ingredients ready while you boil the water and cook the spaghetti.

INGREDIENTS

¾ pound spaghetti

2 ripe avocados, peeled and pitted

1 bunch green onions (white and green parts), roughly chopped

1 medium garlic clove, peeled and chopped

Zest and juice of 1 large lemon

2 tablespoons chopped fresh Italian parsley

2 teaspoons chopped fresh tarragon

Sea salt and freshly ground black pepper, to taste

2 tablespoons extra-virgin olive oil

2 tablespoons cannaoil

1 pound cleaned and cooked jumbo lump crab

1 tablespoon freshly grated Parmesan cheese, plus more for serving

1 small lemon, cut into wedges, for serving

PROCEDURE

1. Bring a large pot of salted water to a boil for the spaghetti.
2. Prepare the pasta according to the package directions. Drain, reserving ¼ cup of pasta water.
3. In the bowl of a food processor fitted with the metal blade, pulse the avocados, green onions, garlic, lemon zest and juice, parsley, tarragon, salt, and pepper until they become a smooth paste. With the machine running, add the olive oil and cannaoil in a steady stream through the feed tube. If the sauce is too stiff, add the reserved pasta water, 1 tablespoon at a time, to thin it out.
4. Put the spaghetti in a large bowl and toss it with the avocado sauce, crab, and Parmesan.
5. Serve topped with a dusting of Parmesan and squeeze of lemon juice.

CHEFS' NOTES

You can easily swap out the crab for cooked shrimp, seared salmon or bass, or whatever looks freshest at the market that day.

To make a Mexican-inspired dish, use cilantro in place of the tarragon and cotija cheese instead of the Parmesan. Seed and chop one jalapeño and add it to the avocado sauce. Top with halved cherry tomatoes and toss with grilled chicken or steak in place of the crab.

MICROWAVE ASPARAGUS AND LEMON RISOTTO

When asparagus is in season, risotto is a great way to showcase it. Traditional risotto can be a somewhat time-consuming affair. But we've discovered a microwave version that requires less stirring and comes together much more quickly.

MAKES:

4 servings

DIFFICULTY:

Easy

INGREDIENTS

1 medium onion, chopped

2 tablespoons butter

1 tablespoon extra-virgin olive oil

1 garlic clove, minced

1 cup arborio rice

3 cups unsalted chicken stock

⅓ cup dry white wine

1 pound asparagus, tough ends removed, cut into ½-inch pieces

½ teaspoon freshly grated lemon zest

1½ tablespoons freshly squeezed lemon juice

½ teaspoon salt (kosher or sea)

¼ teaspoon freshly ground black pepper

4 teaspoons cannabutter

⅓ cup freshly grated Parmigiano-Reggiano cheese, divided

PROCEDURE

1. Combine the onion, butter, olive oil, and garlic in a 2-quart microwave-safe bowl. Microwave on high power for 3 minutes.
2. Stir in the rice and microwave on high for 3 minutes. Stir in the stock and wine and microwave on high for 16 minutes, stirring for 30 seconds every 4 minutes.
3. Stir in asparagus and microwave on high for 3 minutes. Stir in the lemon zest and juice, salt, pepper, cannabutter, and half of the Parmigiano-Reggiano. All the liquid should be absorbed and the rice should be al dente. Top with the remaining cheese and serve immediately.

CHEFS' NOTES

Form any leftover risotto into patties and pan-fry until they are golden brown on each side.

To make this dish vegetarian, substitute vegetable stock for the chicken stock.

Entrées

TURKEY MEATBALLS

This recipe came to Laurie from her friend Freddi and was inspired by one of Mario Batali's dishes. They're now our go-to meatballs—we eat them by themselves, add them to pasta, or put them in a sliced baguette and top them with provolone cheese for a meatball sub.

MAKES:

2 dozen meatballs

SERVING SIZE:

2 meatballs

DIFFICULTY:

Easy

INGREDIENTS

10 slices day-old white bread

2 pounds ground turkey

½ pound bulk Italian sausage

¼ pound prosciutto, diced

4 eggs

½ cup freshly grated Romano cheese

½ cup chopped fresh parsley

4 tablespoons canna-olive oil

2 tablespoons olive oil

Salt (kosher or sea) and freshly ground black pepper, to taste

2 cups Tomato Sauce (page 127)

PROCEDURE

1. Put the bread in a large bowl and cover it with water. Let the bread soften for 5 minutes, then drain it well, using your hands to get as much of the water out as possible.
2. In a large bowl, thoroughly combine the bread, turkey, sausage, and prosciutto. Add the eggs, Romano, parsley, canna-olive oil, olive oil, salt, and pepper and mix well.
3. Refrigerate the meatball mixture for 30 minutes. Preheat the oven to 340°F and line 2 baking sheets with parchment paper.
4. Form the mixture into golf-ball-size meatballs and put them on the baking sheets. They will be a little flat at the bottom, but that's okay.
5. Bake the meatballs until they are firm and golden brown, about 40 minutes.
6. Warm the tomato sauce over medium-low heat.
7. Toss the meatballs with the warm tomato sauce.

OVEN-ROASTED CHICKEN THIGHS WITH GREEN CHILI SAUCE

MAKES:
4 servings

SERVING SIZE:
2 thighs and
¼ cup sauce

DIFFICULTY:
Easy

We have a secret to share: chicken thighs are the unsung heroes of the poultry world. They're inexpensive, very difficult to overcook, and have lots more flavor than a chicken breast. We call for bone-in thighs here but boneless and skinless thighs would work as well.

INGREDIENTS

Vegetable oil

8 bone-in chicken thighs

Cooking spray, for coating chicken

Kosher salt and coarsely ground fresh black pepper

1 cup Green Chili Sauce (below)

2 cups cooked white rice

1 cup cotija cheese

¼ cup chopped fresh cilantro leaves

PROCEDURE

1. Preheat the oven to 425°F. Line a baking sheet with aluminum foil. Place a wire rack on top of the foil.
2. Dry the chicken thighs with a paper towel, trim any excess fat around the edges, and put them on the rack. Spray them with cooking spray, and season with salt and pepper.
3. Roast until an instant-read thermometer inserted into the thickest part of the meat (avoid the bone) registers between 180°F and 185°F, about 35 minutes.
4. Remove the chicken from the oven and let it rest for 5 minutes before serving.
5. While the chicken rests, warm the sauce in a small saucepan over low heat.
6. Serve the chicken thighs over the rice, topped with the sauce, cotija, and cilantro.

GREEN CHILI SAUCE

This sauce is great as a topping for any type of cooked or grilled meat, or even tofu.

INGREDIENTS

5 medium tomatillos, husked

3 whole garlic cloves, unpeeled

2 whole shallots, peeled

1 Roma tomato, halved and seeded

1 whole jalapeño

2 tablespoons grape-seed oil

1 tablespoon salt (kosher or sea)

½ cup roughly chopped fresh cilantro (leaves and stems)

1 tablespoon honey

Zest of 1 lime

Juice of ½ lime

2 teaspoons freshly ground black pepper

3½ tablespoons cannaoil

PROCEDURE

1. Preheat the oven to 400°F.
2. In a large bowl, toss the tomatillos, garlic, shallots, tomato, and jalapeño with the grape-seed oil until the vegetables are coated. Add the salt and toss again.
3. Transfer the vegetables to a baking sheet and roast, turning the vegetables halfway through the process, until they are charred and soft, 18 to 20 minutes. Remove the vegetables from the oven and let them cool.
4. When the vegetables are cool, slice the top off the jalapeño pepper, remove the skins from the garlic, and transfer the vegetables to the bowl of a food processor fitted with the metal blade.
5. Add the cilantro, honey, lime zest, juice, and pepper and pulse a few times to blend.
6. With the machine running, add the cannaoil in a steady stream through the feed tube. Stop and adjust the seasonings, adding more salt and pepper if desired. Pulse until the sauce has the consistency of a thick puree. If needed, add 1 tablespoon water to thin the sauce.

MAKES:
2½ cups sauce

SERVING SIZE:
¼ cup sauce

DIFFICULTY:
Easy

CHICKEN "HENZEL" STYLE

Roost, in Portland, Oregon, is Laurie's favorite restaurant. Megan Henzel is the chef and owner, and some version of this delicious chicken preparation is always on her menu. She doesn't add cannabis, though—at least not yet!

MAKES:

4 servings

DIFFICULTY:

Intermediate

INGREDIENTS

4 chicken breasts

Salt (kosher or sea) and freshly ground black pepper

4 tablespoons olive oil, divided

4 teaspoons canna-olive oil

2 links chorizo, sliced

2 cups peasant bread, cut into cubes of 1½ inches

2 garlic cloves, thinly sliced

1 cup cherry tomatoes

4 cups fresh spinach

PROCEDURE

1. Preheat the oven to 400°F.
2. Season the chicken breasts generously with salt and pepper.
3. In a medium skillet over medium heat, heat 3 tablespoons of the olive oil and sear the breasts on all sides, 5 to 6 minutes total. It is best to cook two at a time rather than crowd the skillet.
4. When all the breasts have been seared, put them on a baking sheet. Bake them until cooked through, 12 to 15 minutes or until the thickest part of the breast registers between 165°F and 170°F on an instant thermometer.
5. Return the skillet to medium heat and add the remaining 1 tablespoon olive oil and the canna-olive oil. Sauté the chorizo until it is beginning to brown, 6–7 minutes.
6. Add the bread cubes and sauté until golden, 5 minutes more.
7. Add the garlic and cherry tomatoes and sauté until garlic is fragrant and the tomatoes begin to soften, about 2 to 3 minutes. The bread and vegetables should be coated with the fat rendered from the chorizo.
8. Add the spinach and cook until it wilts and releases its liquid, 7 to 9 minutes.
9. Divide the bread mixture among 4 plates and top each one with a chicken breast.

ORANGE SESAME CHICKEN

MAKES:

4 servings

DIFFICULTY:

**Intermediate/
Advanced**

Sesame chicken is one of our favorite picks for Chinese takeout—but the chicken is fried and doused in a sauce loaded with sugar and salt. Our make-at-home version uses sautéed chicken instead, bringing all the same great flavors to the table, but with far fewer calories.

INGREDIENTS

1½ pounds boneless and skinless chicken thighs

2 tablespoons low-sodium soy sauce, divided

2 tablespoons canola oil, divided

1 green bell pepper, seeded and cut into thin strips

1 poblano chile, seeded and cut into thin strips

1 carrot, sliced diagonally

½ red onion, thinly sliced

2 garlic cloves, minced

1 tablespoon grated fresh ginger

2 tablespoons hoisin sauce

2 tablespoons freshly squeezed orange juice

1 tablespoon cannaoil

1 tablespoon rice wine vinegar

1½ teaspoons cornstarch blended with ¼ cup water

1 teaspoon toasted sesame oil

4 cups cooked white rice

1 tablespoon black sesame seeds

2 teaspoons freshly grated orange zest

¼ teaspoon red pepper flakes

1 green onion (white and green parts), chopped, for garnish

PROCEDURE

1. Cut the chicken thighs into bite-sized pieces all roughly the same size.

2. Put the chicken pieces in a large bowl, add 1 tablespoon of the soy sauce, and marinate for at least 15 minutes in the refrigerator.

3. While the chicken marinates, heat 1 tablespoon of the canola oil in a large nonstick skillet over medium-high heat. Add the bell pepper, chile, carrot, and onion, and sauté until crisp-tender, 2 to 4 minutes. Remove the vegetables to a plate and set them aside. Do not wash the skillet.

4. In a medium bowl, thoroughly whisk together the garlic, ginger, remaining 1 tablespoon soy sauce, hoisin sauce, orange juice, cannaoil, vinegar, cornstarch-water mixture, and sesame oil. Set the sauce aside.

5. Return the skillet to the heat and heat the remaining 1 tablespoon canola oil over medium heat. Working in 2 batches if necessary, so as not to crowd the pan, add the marinated chicken pieces, and cook until almost done (90 percent of the way), 4 to 5 minutes, depending on the size of your chicken. Check doneness by slicing a piece open. The center should be slightly pink.

6. If working in batches, return all of the cooked chicken to the pan. Reduce the heat to low and add the vegetables and sauce to the chicken. Cook until the sauce thickens, enough to coat the back of a spoon, and the chicken is completely cooked, about 4 minutes.

7. To serve, spoon the chicken and sauce mixture over the rice and top with the sesame seeds, orange zest, and red pepper flakes. Garnish with the green onion.

TOMAHAWK RIB EYE

The tomahawk rib eye (also called a cowboy rib eye) is a rib steak with the entire rib bone left intact. The bone is trimmed of meat and fat, making for an impressive presentation (and it can also act as a handle for the steak, if you're so inclined).

INGREDIENTS

1 (18-ounce) bone-in cowboy-cut rib eye, at room temperature

2 tablespoons canola oil

Kosher salt and coarsely ground fresh black pepper

2 teaspoons Garlic-Herb Cannabutter (page 31) or another compound butter of your choosing

PROCEDURE

1. Put a 12-inch cast-iron skillet in the oven and preheat the oven to 500°F.
2. Rub the steak with the oil and season it liberally with salt and pepper.
3. Wearing an oven mitt, carefully remove the hot skillet from the oven and put it on the stove over high heat. Put the steak in the pan and sear it for 1 minute, then turn it and sear on the other side for 1 minute. Flip the steak and carefully return the pan to the oven.
4. Cook the steak for 3 minutes, flip it, and cook for an additional 3 minutes, or until an instant-read thermometer reads 140°F. Remove it from the oven and let it rest, tented with aluminum foil, for 10 minutes.
5. Slice meat off the bone and cut into thick slices. Top with cannabutter.

SEARED SIRLOIN WITH SAVORY BREAD PUDDING

Good aged balsamic vinegar has great body and a complex sweetness that makes this sirloin sing. But the best part of this dish is the savory bread pudding on the side. Cooking the steaks on a wire rack in the oven allows the air to circulate evenly around them.

MAKES:

4 servings

SERVING SIZE:

1 steak and 1 bread pudding

DIFFICULTY:

Advanced

CHEFS' NOTES:

The leftover bread puddings can be stored, in an airtight bag, in the refrigerator for 4 days. One way to use the bread pudding is to crumble them up and add them to a breakfast hash. You can also cut them in half and top with sausage gravy and poached eggs for a creative twist for breakfast. Or for lunch try cutting them in half, top with butter, and toast in a skillet. Once it's toasted make a slider-size sandwich with sliced country ham, pickle chips, and honey mustard.

INGREDIENTS

For the bread pudding:
Cooking spray, for greasing the pan

1 tablespoon unsalted butter

1 teaspoon vegetable oil

1 stalk celery, chopped

2 tablespoons chopped celery leaves

1 white onion, diced

4 ounces cremini mushrooms

3 tablespoons diced water chestnuts

2 teaspoons garlic-and-herb seasoning blend

½ teaspoon packed brown sugar

2 teaspoons salt (kosher or sea)

1 teaspoon freshly ground black pepper

3 tablespoons cannabutter

½ cup buttermilk

1 cup low-sodium chicken stock

6 ounces plain bread stuffing cubes

For the sirloin:
4 (5-ounce) sirloin steaks, at room temperature

4 tablespoons olive oil

Kosher salt and coarsely ground fresh black pepper

Aged balsamic vinegar, for drizzling

Sea salt, for sprinkling

Chopped cilantro, for garnish

Chopped green onion tops, for garnish

PROCEDURE

Make the bread pudding:

1. Preheat the oven to 340°F.
2. Spray a standard-size muffin pan with cooking spray and set it aside.
3. In a large saucepan, melt the butter with the vegetable oil over medium heat. Add celery, celery leaves, and onion and cook until translucent, 2 to 3 minutes.
4. Add the mushrooms and cook until the liquid has evaporated, about 6 minutes more.
5. Stir in the water chestnuts, spice blend, brown sugar, salt, and pepper.
6. Slowly add the cannabutter, buttermilk, and stock, mixing thoroughly.
7. Put the stuffing in a large bowl and pour the vegetable mixture over it. Thoroughly combine the stuffing and vegetables.
8. Distribute the stuffing evenly among the cups of the prepared muffin pan (it should make 10 muffins).
9. Bake the bread puddings until they are golden brown, 25 to 28 minutes, rotating the pan once halfway through baking.
10. Remove the pan from the oven, tent it with aluminum foil to keep the bread puddings warm while you prepare the steaks, and increase the heat to 400°F.

Make the sirloin:

11. Dry the steaks with paper towels. Rub each steak with 1 tablespoon of olive oil and season liberally with salt and pepper. Put a wire rack on a baking sheet and set it aside.
12. Heat a large cast-iron skillet over medium/high heat. Cook the steaks 2 at a time to avoid overcrowding, for 3 minutes on one side. Turn the steaks and cook for 3 minutes on the other side.
13. Put the steaks on the wire rack on the prepared baking sheet. Cook the steaks to the desired degree of doneness: 3 to 5 minutes for medium rare, 5 to 7 for medium, 8 to 9 for medium well. If the pan is not large enough to comfortably hold the steaks, prepare in batches.
14. Transfer the steaks to a cutting board and let them rest, tented with aluminum foil, for 5 minutes.
15. Drizzle the steaks with balsamic vinegar, sprinkle with sea salt, and top with the cilantro and green onion. Serve them alongside the bread pudding.

GAUCHO GRILLED STEAK WITH CHIMICHURRI

MAKES:

8 servings

DIFFICULTY:

Easy

Chimichurri is a strongly flavored, brightly colored Argentinian condiment made from parsley and garlic. It's typically served with grilled steak, but it's also delectable on chicken, fish, or pork, or as a marinade, which is how we use it in this recipe.

INGREDIENTS

2 pounds skirt steak, fat trimmed

1 cup Chimichurri (recipe below)

PROCEDURE

1. Combine the steak with the chimichurri in a large zip-top plastic bag. Marinate in the refrigerator for 3 hours.
2. Prepare a gas or charcoal grill for medium heat. Discard the marinade, and grill the steak medium rare, 4 to 5 minutes a side.
3. Let the steak rest for 10 minutes, tented with aluminum foil, before slicing it against the grain. Serve it hot or at room temperature.

CHIMICHURRI

If you'd like an extra dose, double this recipe: use one portion of chimichurri as the marinade and serve the other alongside the steak.

INGREDIENTS

1 bunch Italian parsley, chopped

6 cloves garlic, chopped

2 tablespoons plus 2 teaspoons cannaoil

½ cup olive oil

¼ cup red wine vinegar

1 tablespoon chopped red onion

2 teaspoons freshly squeezed lemon juice

1 teaspoon dried oregano

½ teaspoon salt (kosher or sea)

Freshly ground black pepper, to taste

PROCEDURE

1. In the bowl of a food processor fitted with the metal blade, pulse all the ingredients until pureed.

MAKES:
1 cup chimichurri

SERVING SIZE:
2 tablespoons chimichurri

DIFFICULTY:
Easy

STUFFED SOLE

Sole is a mild, delicate fish that's a good choice for people who don't usually love seafood. In this recipe, the fish is wrapped around a creamy, crunchy shrimp filling.

MAKES:
4 servings

SERVING SIZE:
2 fillets

DIFFICULTY:
Intermediate

INGREDIENTS

8 (3-ounce) sole fillets

½ cup mayonnaise

¼ cup raw bay shrimp

2 tablespoons panko bread crumbs

4 teaspoons cannabutter

1 teaspoon chopped onion

1 green onion (white and green parts), finely chopped

1 teaspoon Worcestershire sauce

Pinch of garlic salt

4 teaspoons Rémoulade Cannabutter (page 31)

PROCEDURE

1. Preheat the oven to 325°F.
2. Make a slit about 2 inches long in the center of 4 of the fillets.
3. In a small bowl, thoroughly combine the mayonnaise, shrimp, bread crumbs, cannabutter, onion, green onion, Worcestershire sauce, and garlic salt.
4. Divide the stuffing mixture into 4 equal portions. Turn the 4 uncut fillets over so that the gray side is facing up. Place the stuffing in the center of 4 pieces. Top with the remaining pieces gray side down, making sure that the slit is centered over the stuffing. Now tuck the pieces of sole under, like making a bed with 2 sheets. Put the fish packages on a rimmed, nonstick baking sheet.
5. Top each package with 1 teaspoon of the rémoulade cannabutter.
6. Bake until the stuffing is cooked and the fish flakes easily, about 20 minutes.

CIOPPINO

Cioppino is an Italian-American stew that originated in San Francisco in the late 1800s. It was originally made by fishermen to use up their catch of the day; we recommend you use whatever fish and shellfish looks best at the market. Serve with pita or bagel chips or croutons, and pass the hot sauce!

INGREDIENTS

1 tablespoon cannaoil

1 medium onion, cut into wedges

3 garlic cloves, mashed

1 (28-ounce) can crushed tomatoes

1 (8-ounce) jar clam juice

¼ cup full-bodied red wine, such as a cabernet or pinot noir

1 pound assorted fish of your choosing, skinned and cut into chunks

½ cup shucked mussels

PROCEDURE

1. In a large saucepan, heat the cannaoil over medium-low heat. Sauté the onion and garlic until translucent, 4 to 6 minutes.
2. Reduce the heat to low. Add the tomatoes, clam juice, and wine and simmer until hot, 12 to 15 minutes.
3. Add the fish and mussels and simmer until the fish is cooked through, 5 to 7 minutes. Serve hot.

ROASTED COD ON ARUGULA PUREE

MAKES:

4 servings

DIFFICULTY:

Easy

The crunchy coating on the cod here makes for an appealing contrast against the zesty arugula puree. If cod isn't available, this technique works well with many types of fish, including salmon and Dover sole. Whichever fish you use, take care not to overcook it or the magic will be lost.

INGREDIENTS

For the cod:
4 (6-ounce) cod fillets

Salt (kosher or sea) and freshly ground black pepper, to taste

4 tablespoons mayonnaise

½ cup panko bread crumbs

2 garlic cloves, minced

2 tablespoons chopped fresh Italian parsley

For the arugula puree:
7 cups arugula, packed

⅓ cup olive oil

4 teaspoons canna-olive oil

2 tablespoons freshly grated Parmesan cheese

1 tablespoon freshly squeezed lemon juice

1 garlic clove, minced

Salt (kosher or sea) and freshly ground black pepper, to taste

PROCEDURE

Make the cod:
1. Preheat the oven to 400°F.
2. Put the cod fillets on an oiled baking sheet. Season them with salt and pepper. Spread 1 tablespoon of mayonnaise over each fillet.
3. In a small bowl, thoroughly combine the bread crumbs, garlic, and parsley and sprinkle evenly over the fish. Set aside.
4. Bake the fish until it flakes easily, 8 to 10 minutes.

Make the arugula puree:
5. In a blender or food processor, puree all the ingredients.
6. Divide the arugula puree among 4 plates, lay a fillet on top of the puree in the center, and serve immediately.

CHEFS' NOTES

The puree is also wonderful on ripe tomatoes, on sandwiches, or tossed with your favorite pasta.

If arugula is too peppery for you, feel free to substitute spinach.

Drinks

MEXICAN HOT CHOCOLATE

Rich, spicy, and elegant, this hot chocolate is one of our favorite indulgences. And it's not just for winter—we drink it year-round. For extra glam, top it with whipped cream and serve it with a cinnamon stick for stirring.

MAKES:
2 servings

DIFFICULTY:
Easy

INGREDIENTS

6 tablespoons dark chocolate hot cocoa mix

1½ tablespoons chocolate syrup

2 teaspoons cannabutter, at room temperature

2 small pinches of chili powder (optional)

½ cup whole milk, heated until warm to the touch

1½ cups water, heated until warm to the touch

¼ teaspoon ground cinnamon or 2 pinches of cayenne pepper, for garnish

PROCEDURE

1. In a saucepan, whisk together the cocoa mix, chocolate syrup, canna-butter, and chili powder, if using, over medium-low heat until the butter has melted and the mix has dissolved.
2. Pour the warmed milk into the pan and whisk until well combined.
3. Pour the warmed water into the pan and whisk to combine. Reduce the heat to low, and warm the chocolate until hot, 2 to 3 minutes.
4. Divide the hot chocolate between 2 mugs, and garnish each mug with ¼ teaspoon cinnamon. Serve immediately.

CHEFS' NOTES

Garnish with a candy cane or chocolate-mint candy, such as a York Peppermint Pattie, instead of the cinnamon, for a holiday treat.

For a double dose, substitute Chocolate Sauce (page 233) for the chocolate syrup.

GOLDEN DELIGHT

While working on this book, we met a lovely young woman named Erica, and she shared this drink recipe with us. It was so scrumptious, we couldn't resist passing it on. As an added bonus, coconut milk, cinnamon, honey, and turmeric contain powerful antioxidants. Thank you, Erica!

MAKES:

2 servings

DIFFICULTY:

Easy

INGREDIENTS

2½ cups coconut milk

3 tablespoons honey

1½ teaspoons curry powder

½ teaspoon ground turmeric

¼ teaspoon ground cinnamon

2 teaspoons cannabutter

PROCEDURE

1. Put all the ingredients except the cannabutter in a blender and blend on medium speed until smooth.
2. Pour the liquid into a medium saucepan and heat, stirring occasionally, over medium-low heat, until very warm but not simmering, 5 to 7 minutes.
3. Divide the mixture between 2 mugs, topping each with 1 teaspoon of cannabutter. Serve immediately.

GREEN & OH-SO-GROOVY SMOOTHIE

MAKES:

2 servings

DIFFICULTY:

Easy

Green juices are all the rage right now. This smoothie is high in essential nutrients, and the addition of avocado (also healthy) makes it smooth and creamy. If you like your smoothies extra-frosty, throw a few ice cubes in the blender along with the rest of the ingredients.

INGREDIENTS

2 ripe avocados, peeled and pitted

1 cup water

1 tablespoon freshly squeezed lemon juice

1 cup packed fresh spinach

½ cup packed fresh cilantro

2 tablespoons freshly squeezed lime juice

2 tablespoons agave nectar

2 teaspoons canna-coconut oil

PROCEDURE

1. Put the avocados in a blender along with the water and lemon juice. Blend on medium speed until smooth.
2. Add the remaining ingredients and blend well. Divide the smoothie between 2 glasses.

CHEFS' NOTE

Substitute any kind of kale (stemmed and chopped) for the spinach.

VERY, VERY BERRY SMOOTHIE

MAKES:

2 servings

DIFFICULTY:

Easy

We love smoothies. Strawberries and bananas are a classic smoothie combination, and we've also added raspberries and coconut milk to further tantalize your taste buds. If you don't have coconut milk on hand, the same amount of plain yogurt is a fine substitute.

INGREDIENTS

1½ cups coconut milk

½ cup freshly squeezed orange juice (from 2 medium oranges)

2 cups hulled, sliced strawberries plus 2 whole strawberries, for garnish

1 cup raspberries

1 small banana, sliced

2 teaspoons canna-coconut oil

PROCEDURE

1. Put all the ingredients in a blender and blend on medium speed until smooth.
2. Divide the smoothie between 2 glasses and garnish each with a strawberry.

DATE MARTINI SMOOTHIE

Laurie's husband, Bruce, suggested serving this sweet, nutty smoothie in a martini glass, complete with a garnish on the rim. It makes the drink extra fun and fabulous, though any glass will work.

MAKES:

2 servings

DIFFICULTY:

Easy

INGREDIENTS

2 cups almond milk

12 pitted dates

1 small banana, sliced

½ cup almond butter

2 teaspoons cannaoil

¼ cup honey or maple syrup, divided

¼ cup finely chopped almonds

PROCEDURE

1. Put the almond milk, dates, banana, almond butter, cannaoil, and 2 tablespoons of the honey in a blender.
2. Put the remaining 2 tablespoons honey on a small plate.
3. Put the almonds on a separate plate.
4. Roll the rim of a martini glass through the honey or syrup, followed by the almonds. Repeat the process if necessary until the rim is completely coated. Repeat with the second glass.
5. Blend the smoothie on medium speed until smooth, and carefully pour into the glasses (you will have some left over). Keep the leftovers in the fridge and blend again to enjoy twice.

MALTED-CHOCOLATE SMOOTHIE

This drink is like a chocolate-covered malt ball in smoothie form. If you want a smoothie with an increased dose, use our Chocolate Sauce (page 233) in place of the chocolate syrup.

MAKES:
2 servings

DIFFICULTY:
Easy

INGREDIENTS

2 cups chocolate milk

1 small banana, sliced

2 tablespoons malted milk powder

1 tablespoon unsweetened cocoa powder

2 teaspoons canna-coconut oil

2 heaping tablespoons chocolate syrup

PROCEDURE

1. Put all the ingredients except the chocolate syrup in a blender. Blend on medium speed until smooth.
2. Divide the smoothie between 2 glasses and stir 1 heaping tablespoon of chocolate syrup into each.

CHEFS' NOTE

If you're not a fan of malt flavor, you can omit the malted milk powder, and you'll get something that tastes more like a chocolate milkshake.

MANGO-CANTALOUPE SMOOTHIE

The combination of mango, cantaloupe, and coconut is divine. For the best-tasting result, use the ripest, most fragrant fruit you can find.

INGREDIENTS

1½ cups coconut milk

1 medium-sized mango, peeled, pitted, and cut into chunks

1 small banana, sliced

1 cup cantaloupe chunks

2 tablespoons agave nectar or honey

2 teaspoons canna-coconut oil

Pinch of cinnamon

PROCEDURE

1. Put all the ingredients in a blender and blend on medium speed until smooth.
2. Divide the smoothie between 2 glasses.

PISTACHIO-LIME SMOOTHIE

Based on personal experience, Melissa has found that pistachios and citrus are helpful in bringing her back down to earth when she's overindulged in cannabis. Pistachios are high in protein, fiber, and essential vitamins such as B6, so whether you had too much the night before or just want a delicious pick-me-up, give this nutty green smoothie a try.

MAKES:

2 servings

DIFFICULTY:

Easy

INGREDIENTS

1½ cups almond milk

1 ripe avocado, peeled and pitted

1 small banana, sliced

1 whole lime, cut in chunks

¼ cup freshly squeezed lime juice (from 2 large limes) or concentrate

¼ cup shelled, unsalted pistachios plus 1 tablespoon chopped pistachios, for garnish

2 to 4 tablespoons honey (depending on how sweet you want it)

2 teaspoons canna-coconut oil

PROCEDURE

1. Put all the ingredients except for the chopped pistachios in a blender and blend on medium speed until smooth.
2. Divide the smoothie between 2 glasses and garnish each with ½ tablespoon of pistachios.

Baked Goods

GRANOLA

Homemade granola tastes so much better than store-bought, and you can customize it to your specific tastes!
The recipe below includes our favorite granola ingredients, but feel free to switch things up: try pecans instead of
walnuts, raisins instead of dried cherries, and cardamom or nutmeg instead of cinnamon.

MAKES:

2 cups granola

SERVING SIZE:

¹/₃ cup granola

DIFFICULTY:

Easy

INGREDIENTS

1½ cups rolled oats

¼ cup chopped walnuts

¼ cup shredded unsweetened coconut

2 tablespoons dried chopped cherries

2 tablespoons whole flaxseed

2 tablespoons canna-coconut oil, melted

2 tablespoons honey

½ teaspoon ground cinnamon

PROCEDURE

1. Preheat the oven to 300°F.
2. Put all the ingredients in a large bowl and toss together well. Taste and add more honey or cinnamon, if desired.
3. Spread the granola in one layer on a rimmed baking sheet.
4. Bake, stirring every 10 minutes, until golden brown, about 30 minutes. Let the granola cool on the baking sheet—it will be soft when it first comes out of the oven but will crisp up as it cools.

BLACK PEPPER DROP BISCUITS

Drop biscuits are very easy to make—there's no rolling out and cutting involved. These biscuits are light, fluffy, and savory with a hint of black pepper. They freeze well, so feel free to double the recipe.

MAKES:
20 small biscuits

SERVING SIZE:
1 biscuit

DIFFICULTY:
Intermediate

INGREDIENTS

1½ cups all-purpose flour

1½ tablespoons coarsely ground fresh black pepper

2 teaspoons baking powder

1 teaspoon salt (kosher or sea)

6 tablespoons cold unsalted butter, cut into small cubes

2 tablespoons cold cannabutter, cut into small cubes

¾ cup buttermilk

1 tablespoon unsalted butter, melted

PROCEDURE

1. Preheat the oven to 340°F and line a baking sheet with parchment paper.
2. Put the flour, pepper, baking powder, and salt in the bowl of a food processor fitted with the metal blade or in a large bowl. Whisk or pulse to combine.
3. Add both cold butters to the flour mixture. Pulse in the food processor, or cut the butter into the flour with a pastry cutter or 2 knives, until the mixture resembles coarse meal.
4. Slowly add the buttermilk and pulse or stir with a fork until the dough just comes together. It will be tacky.
5. Scoop heaping tablespoons of dough onto the prepared baking sheet, leaving 2 inches between scoops.
6. Bake the biscuits until golden brown, 15 to 20 minutes. Remove them from the oven and brush the tops with the melted butter.
7. Transfer biscuits to a wire rack to cool slightly before serving (they're also delicious at room temperature).

CHEFS' NOTE

To up the dosage, serve our Strawberry Sauce (page 235) alongside the warm biscuits.

ORANGE CRANBERRY WALNUT BISCOTTI

MAKES:
20 biscotti

SERVING SIZE:
2 biscotti

DIFFICULTY:
Intermediate

Making biscotti takes a bit of time, since the dough is shaped into loaves and baked, then cooled, sliced, and baked again (in fact, the word "biscotti" comes from a Latin term meaning "twice-baked"). But these crunchy cookies are worth the work; they make a great breakfast or afternoon snack.

INGREDIENTS

2 cups all-purpose flour

²⁄₃ cup sugar plus ¼ cup for sprinkling the biscotti (optional)

1 teaspoon baking powder

¼ teaspoon salt (kosher or sea)

2 eggs, lightly beaten, plus one egg white for glazing the biscotti (optional)

2 teaspoons vanilla extract

3 tablespoons plus 1 teaspoon cannaoil

1 tablespoon orange juice concentrate

1 tablespoon freshly grated orange zest

1 cup chopped walnuts

½ cup dried cranberries

PROCEDURE

1. Preheat the oven to 340°F and have 2 ungreased baking sheets handy.
2. In a large bowl, whisk together the flour, sugar, baking powder, and salt.
3. In a small bowl, whisk together the eggs, vanilla, cannaoil, orange juice concentrate, and zest.
4. Add the wet ingredients to the dry ingredients and mix just until the flour is moistened.
5. Fold in the walnuts and cranberries and gently knead the dough with floured hands until mixed.
6. Divide the dough in half and, again using floured hands, pat each half into two 10-by-2½-inch logs.
7. Put each log on a baking sheet and bake until they are golden brown, 20 to 25 minutes, rotating sheets once halfway through baking. Keep the oven on.
8. Transfer the logs to a wire rack and cool them for 10 minutes.
9. Transfer the cooled logs to a cutting board and, using a serrated knife, slice them on the diagonal into 1-inch slices.
10. Put the biscotti back on the baking sheets. If you like, brush each with the egg white and sprinkle with sugar.
11. Bake the biscotti until light golden brown, 8 to 10 minutes on each side, or a little longer if you like a crisper biscotti.
12. Transfer the biscotti to wire racks to cool completely.

HARVEST MUFFINS

MAKES:

1 dozen muffins

SERVING SIZE:

1 muffin

DIFFICULTY:

Easy

These rustic, satisfying muffins are chock-full of fruit and nuts. We like to use paper liners when we bake muffins (and cupcakes, too)—that way, nothing sticks to the muffin tins.

INGREDIENTS

Cooking spray, for greasing the liners

2 eggs

½ cup canola oil

¼ cup canna-canola oil

¼ cup milk

1 cup all-purpose flour

1 cup whole-wheat flour

1 cup packed brown sugar

2 teaspoons baking soda

1 teaspoon ground cinnamon

½ teaspoon salt (kosher or sea)

1½ cups shredded carrots (2 to 3 medium carrots)

1½ cups shredded peeled apples (we like Granny Smith)

¾ cup chopped walnuts

½ cup shredded unsweetened coconut

½ cup raisins

PROCEDURE

1. Preheat the oven to 340°F. Line a standard-size muffin tin with paper liners, spray the liners with the cooking spray, and set the pan aside.
2. In a medium mixing bowl, beat together the eggs, canola oil, canna-canola oil, and milk.
3. In a large bowl, whisk together the all-purpose flour, whole-wheat flour, brown sugar, baking soda, cinnamon, and salt.
4. Add the wet ingredients to the dry ingredients, mixing well.
5. Add the remaining ingredients and mix well.
6. Spoon the batter into the prepared liners, filling each three-quarters full. Bake the muffins until the tops are firm and set and a toothpick comes out clean, 30 to 35 minutes.
7. Cool in the pan for 10 minutes before removing to a wire rack to cool completely.

STRAWBERRY STREUSEL MUFFINS

Crumbly, buttery streusel topping takes plain baked goods to a new level. Using plump, juicy, in-season strawberries makes these muffins especially delightful.

MAKES:
1 dozen muffins

SERVING SIZE:
1 muffin

DIFFICULTY:
Easy

INGREDIENTS

For the muffins:
Cooking spray, for greasing the paper liners

2 eggs, lightly beaten

½ cup almond milk

½ cup sour cream

3 tablespoons canola oil

2 tablespoons cannaoil

2¼ cups all-purpose flour

⅓ cup sugar

2 teaspoons baking powder

¼ teaspoon salt (kosher or sea)

1½ cups hulled, chopped fresh strawberries

For the streusel topping:
¼ cup all-purpose flour

¼ cup packed brown sugar

½ teaspoon ground cinnamon

2 tablespoons cold cannabutter, cut into small cubes

PROCEDURE

Make the muffins:

1. Preheat the oven to 340°F. Line a standard-size muffin tin with paper liners, spray the liners with the cooking spray, and set the pan aside.
2. In a medium bowl, beat together the eggs, almond milk, sour cream, canola oil, and cannaoil.
3. In a large bowl, whisk together the flour, sugar, baking powder, and salt.
4. Add the wet ingredients to the dry ingredients, mixing well.
5. Gently fold in the berries.
6. Spoon the batter into the prepared liners, filling each three-quarters full.

Make the streusel topping:

7. In a small bowl, combine the flour, brown sugar, and cinnamon. Work the butter into the dry mixture with your hands to form a crumb topping. Top the muffins evenly with the streusel.
8. Bake the muffins until they are golden brown, 20 to 25 minutes.
9. Remove muffins from the tin and cool on a wire rack.

SPELT SCONES

Spelt is an ancient species of wheat that is lately becoming more popular and widely available (in most major grocery stores and online). Its rich, nutty, slightly sweet flavor lends an earthiness to baked goods.

MAKES:

9 scones

SERVING SIZE:

1 scone

DIFFICULTY:

Intermediate

INGREDIENTS

2 cups light spelt flour plus ¼ cup for kneading the dough

¾ cup rolled oats plus ¼ cup for kneading the dough

1 teaspoon ground cinnamon

1 heaping tablespoon baking powder

Pinch of salt (kosher or sea)

3 tablespoons coconut oil

3 tablespoons canna-coconut oil

½ cup maple syrup

½ cup coconut milk, plus more to moisten dough, if needed

PROCEDURE

1. Preheat the oven to 340°F and have a baking sheet handy.
2. In a large bowl, whisk together 2 cups of the spelt flour, ¾ cup of the oatmeal, cinnamon, baking powder, and salt.
3. In the same bowl, with clean fingers, or in the bowl of a food processor fitted with the metal blade, combine or pulse the dry ingredients with the coconut oil and cannaoil until the mixture resembles coarse crumbs.
4. In a small bowl, stir together the ¼ cup spelt flour and ¼ cup oatmeal. Sprinkle the mixture on your work surface.
5. Add the maple syrup and coconut milk to the dough, mixing until the dough just comes together. Add more coconut milk, 2 teaspoons at a time, if the dough is dry.
6. On the prepared work surface, knead the dough for 1 to 2 minutes in the flour/oatmeal mixture until it just comes together. Don't overwork the dough.
7. Pat the dough into a circle about 1 inch thick. Score the dough into 9 wedges.
8. Cut out the wedges and put them on the ungreased baking sheet.
9. Bake until the scones are firm and light golden brown and a toothpick comes out clean, 20 to 25 minutes.
10. Remove to a wire rack to cool.

ALMOND–POPPY SEED SCONES

Gone are the days of dry, bland scones that were simply carriers for butter or jam. These scones are moist and full of flavor, and the poppy seeds provide a wonderful bit of crunch. They are perfect for breakfast, or with a cup of tea for an afternoon snack. Just check your teeth for seeds in the mirror afterward!

INGREDIENTS

For the scones:
2 cups all-purpose flour, plus more for dusting the work surface

½ cup sugar

1 tablespoon poppy seeds

2 teaspoons baking powder

½ teaspoon salt (kosher or sea)

¼ cup cold cannabutter, cut into small or large cubes

¼ cup (½ stick) cold unsalted butter, cut into pieces

⅓ cup vanilla yogurt (non-Greek)

1 egg

1 egg yolk

2 tablespoons milk

1 teaspoon almond extract

For the glaze:
½ cup confectioners' sugar

2 to 4 teaspoons whole milk

¼ teaspoon almond extract

PROCEDURE

Make the scones:

1. Preheat the oven to 340°F. Line 2 baking sheets with parchment paper and set them aside. Dust your work surface with flour.
2. In a large bowl, whisk together the flour, sugar, poppy seeds, baking powder, and salt.
3. Using a pastry cutter or 2 knives, cut in the cannabutter and unsalted butter until the mixture resembles coarse meal.
4. In a small bowl, beat together the yogurt, egg, egg yolk, milk, and almond extract.
5. Add the wet ingredients to the dry ingredients, mixing until the dough just comes together.
6. Knead the dough a few times and divide it into 2 equal balls.
7. Pat the dough balls into 6-inch circles and score each into 6 wedges.
8. Cut out the wedges and put them on the prepared baking sheets. Bake until the scones are firm and golden brown, 12 to 15 minutes.

While the scones bake, make the glaze:

9. In a small bowl whisk together the confectioners' sugar, milk, and almond extract. If it seems too dry, add 1 teaspoon milk.
10. Let the scones cool completely on the baking sheet, then brush them with the glaze. Let the glaze set at least 1 hour before serving.

MAKES:
1 dozen scones

SERVING SIZE:
1 scone

DIFFICULTY:
Intermediate

BANANA BREAD

When we buy bananas, at least one of the bunch usually starts to turn brown before we can get to it. Banana bread to the rescue! We recommend letting your bananas turn fully brown before you bake with them. They'll be extra sweet that way.

MAKES:

12 slices

SERVING SIZE:

1 slice

DIFFICULTY:

Easy

INGREDIENTS

Cooking spray, for greasing the pan

2 cups all-purpose flour

¾ teaspoon baking soda

½ teaspoon salt (kosher or sea)

1 cup sugar

¼ cup raspberry-mint cannabutter, softened

3 overripe bananas, mashed

2 eggs

3 cups chopped pecans

1/3 cup vanilla yogurt (non-Greek)

2 teaspoons vanilla extract

PROCEDURE

1. Preheat the oven to 340°F and spray a 9-by-5-inch loaf pan with the cooking spray. Set it aside.
2. In a medium bowl, whisk together the flour, baking soda, and salt.
3. In a large bowl, beat together the sugar and cannabutter. Stir in the bananas, eggs, pecans, yogurt, and vanilla.
4. Add the dry ingredients to wet ingredients, mixing until just combined.
5. Pour the batter into the prepared pan and bake until the bread is light golden brown and a toothpick inserted in the center comes out clean, 45 to 50 minutes.
6. Let cool for 10 minutes in the pan set on a wire rack before turning out to cool completely on the rack.

ORANGE-PISTACHIO BREAD

Laurie likes this bread so much that she generally makes several loaves at a time and freezes the extras. Full disclosure: it actually tastes really good just out of the freezer.

MAKES:
12 slices

SERVING SIZE:
1 slice

DIFFICULTY:
Easy

INGREDIENTS

Cooking spray, for greasing the pan

1 cup sugar

½ cup canola oil

¼ cup cannaoil

2 eggs, lightly beaten

1 cup buttermilk

2 teaspoons freshly grated orange zest

2½ cups all-purpose flour

1 teaspoon baking soda

½ teaspoon ground cinnamon

Pinch of salt (kosher or sea)

¾ cup chopped shelled, unsalted pistachios

PROCEDURE

1. Preheat the oven to 340°F and spray a 9-by-5-inch loaf pan with the cooking spray. Set it aside.
2. In a large bowl, beat together the sugar, canola oil, and cannaoil until creamy. Add the eggs, buttermilk, and zest, mixing well.
3. In a medium bowl, whisk together the flour, baking soda, cinnamon, and salt.
4. Add the dry ingredients to wet ingredients, mixing until just combined.
5. Fold in the pistachios.
6. Pour the batter into the prepared pan and bake until the bread is golden brown and a toothpick inserted in the center comes out clean, about 50 minutes.
7. Let cool for 10 minutes in the pan set on a wire rack before turning out to cool completely on the rack.

GRIDDLED CORN BREAD WITH YOGURT AND FRUIT

MAKES:

4 servings

DIFFICULTY:

Easy

Growing up in New York, Laurie loved the griddled corn muffins she could get in diners. (She could also get a cup of lousy coffee for a dime.) You can use your favorite corn-bread recipe, or follow ours below. If you use ours, but don't want a double dose of cannabis, simply use regular butter instead of cannabutter for the sautéing.

INGREDIENTS

1 cup vanilla Greek yogurt

1 cup mixed seasonal fruit

2 tablespoons butter

4 teaspoons cannabutter

4 slices Corn Bread (recipe below)

PROCEDURE

1. In a small bowl, stir together the yogurt and fruit and set it aside.
2. In a large nonstick skillet, melt the butter and cannabutter. When the butter foams, add the sliced corn bread and cook until it is light golden brown, 3 to 4 minutes. Flip the bread and cook on the other side until light golden brown, about 3 more minutes.
3. Divide the cornbread among 4 plates, topped with the yogurt mixture.

NEW YORK–STYLE CORN BREAD

There are so many corn bread styles it is hard to have a favorite. We tend to go for the slightly sweeter variety, although the less sweet Southern style certainly has its place.

INGREDIENTS

Cooking spray, for greasing the pan

1½ cups all-purpose flour

¾ cup sugar

½ cup cornmeal

1 tablespoon baking powder

¼ teaspoon salt (kosher or sea)

1⅓ cups milk

2 eggs, lightly beaten

¼ cup canola oil

¼ cup cannabutter, melted

2 tablespoons honey

PROCEDURE

1. Preheat the oven to 340°F and spray an 8-inch square baking pan with cooking spray. Set it aside.
2. In a large bowl, whisk together the flour, sugar, cornmeal, baking powder, and salt.
3. In a medium bowl, whisk together the milk, eggs, canola oil, cannabutter, and honey.
4. Add wet ingredients to the dry ingredients, mixing until just combined.
5. Pour the batter into the prepared pan and bake until golden brown, 30 to 35 minutes.

MAKES:
12 slices

SERVING SIZE:
1 slice

DIFFICULTY:
Easy

Cookies and
Desserts

TRIPLE-CHOCOLATE ESPRESSO COOKIES

Everyone who tastes these cookies begs us for the recipe—it has the perfect cocoa flavor, plus two kinds of chocolate chips and just a hint of espresso.

MAKES:

4 dozen cookies

SERVING SIZE:

2 cookies

DIFFICULTY:

Easy

INGREDIENTS

Cooking spray, for greasing the baking sheets

2 cups all-purpose flour

²⁄₃ cup unsweetened cocoa powder

2 teaspoons instant espresso powder

1 teaspoon baking soda

¼ teaspoon salt (kosher or sea)

½ cup (1 stick) unsalted butter, softened

½ cup (8 tablespoons) cannabutter, softened

1 cup granulated sugar

½ cup packed brown sugar

2 eggs

2 teaspoons vanilla extract

1 cup bittersweet chocolate chips

²⁄₃ cup white chocolate chips

PROCEDURE

1. Preheat the oven to 340°F. Spray 2 baking sheets with cooking spray and set them aside.
2. In a medium bowl, whisk together the flour, cocoa and espresso powders, baking soda, and salt.
3. In the bowl of a stand mixer fitted with the paddle attachment (or use a hand mixer or a wooden spoon in a large bowl), combine the unsalted butter, cannabutter, granulated sugar, and brown sugar. Beat on medium speed until fluffy.
4. Reduce the speed to low and add the eggs and vanilla. Beat until well mixed, about 1 minute.
5. Add the flour mixture and mix until just combined. Stir in the bittersweet and white chocolate chips.
6. Drop the dough by heaping tablespoons onto the prepared baking sheets, about 2 inches apart. Bake until the cookies are set and no longer shiny, 7 to 9 minutes.
7. Remove the cookies from the oven and let them cool on the baking sheets for 2 minutes. Transfer the cookies to a wire rack to cool completely.
8. Repeat with the remaining dough, cooling the baking sheets between batches.
9. Store cookies in an airtight container.

APRICOT CHOCOLATE CHIP COOKIES

We recently had a love affair with chocolate-covered apricots, and chocolate chip cookies are a perennial favorite of ours. The natural next step was to create a recipe that combined both—and it's a winner.

MAKES:

4 dozen cookies

SERVING SIZE:

2 cookies

DIFFICULTY:

Easy

INGREDIENTS

Cooking spray, for greasing the baking sheets

2¼ cups all-purpose flour

1 teaspoon baking soda

½ teaspoon salt (kosher or sea)

1 cup (2 sticks) unsalted butter, softened

½ cup (8 tablespoons) cannabutter, softened

1 cup packed brown sugar

½ cup granulated sugar

2 eggs

2 teaspoons vanilla extract

1 cup semisweet chocolate chips

1 cup bittersweet chocolate chips

1 cup chopped dried apricots

PROCEDURE

1. Preheat the oven to 340°F. Spray 2 baking sheets with cooking spray and set them aside.
2. In a medium bowl, whisk together the flour, baking soda, and salt.
3. In the bowl of a stand mixer fitted with the paddle attachment (or use a hand mixer or a wooden spoon in a large bowl), combine the unsalted butter, cannabutter, brown sugar, and granulated sugar. Beat on medium speed until fluffy.
4. Reduce the speed to low and add the eggs and vanilla. Beat until well mixed, about 1 minute.
5. Add the flour mixture and mix until just combined. Stir in the semisweet and bittersweet chocolate chips and dried apricots.
6. Drop the dough by heaping tablespoons onto the prepared baking sheets, about 2 inches apart. Bake until the cookies are light golden brown, 7 to 9 minutes.
7. Remove the cookies from the oven and let them cool on the baking sheets for 2 minutes. Transfer the cookies to a wire rack to cool completely.
8. Repeat with the remaining dough, cooling the baking sheets between batches.
9. Store cookies in an airtight container.

MATCHA SUGAR COOKIES

MAKES:

4 dozen cookies

SERVING SIZE:

2 cookies

DIFFICULTY:

Intermediate

Matcha is a nutrient-rich powder made from green tea. It figures prominently in the traditional Japanese tea ceremony. By itself, matcha is an acquired taste, but it pairs wonderfully with other flavors, especially in desserts. You can purchase it in gourmet grocery stores or online.

INGREDIENTS

2¾ cups all-purpose flour

1 teaspoon baking soda

½ teaspoon baking powder

¼ teaspoon salt (kosher or sea)

2 teaspoons matcha powder, divided

½ cup (1 stick) unsalted butter, softened

½ cup (8 tablespoons) cannabutter, softened

1½ cups granulated sugar

1 egg

1 teaspoon vanilla extract

4 tablespoons buttermilk, divided

1 cup confectioners' sugar

2 tablespoons milk

Decorations, such as colored dragées

PROCEDURE

1. Preheat the oven to 340°F. Have 2 cookie sheets handy.
2. In a medium bowl, whisk together the flour, baking soda, baking powder, salt, and 1 teaspoon of the matcha powder.
3. In the bowl of a stand mixer fitted with the paddle attachment (or use a hand mixer or a wooden spoon in a large bowl), combine the unsalted butter, cannabutter, and granulated sugar. Beat on medium speed until fluffy.
4. Reduce the speed to low and add the egg, vanilla, and 3 tablespoons of the buttermilk. Beat until well mixed, about 1 minute.
5. Add the flour mixture and mix until just combined.
6. Form the dough into a ball, wrap the ball in plastic wrap, and refrigerate it for 1 hour.
7. Working with pieces of chilled dough, roll them between your palms into 1½-inch balls and place them on the ungreased cookie sheets 2 inches apart.
8. With your palm, flatten the balls and brush the tops with the remaining 1 tablespoon of the buttermilk.
9. Bake until the cookies are light golden brown around the edges, 8 to 10 minutes. Remove the cookies from the oven and let them cool on the baking sheets for 2 minutes. Transfer the cookies to a wire rack to cool completely.
10. Repeat with the remaining dough, cooling the baking sheets between batches.
11. In a small bowl, combine the confectioners' sugar with the milk and remaining 1 teaspoon of the matcha powder, stirring well so there are no lumps. Brush the glaze onto the cooled cookies and decorate.

PEANUT BUTTER THUMBPRINT COOKIES

Peanut butter cookies are delicious on their own. However, by adding chocolate and chocolate toffee bits, you are entering an entirely different plane of goodness.

MAKES:

3 dozen cookies

SERVING SIZE:

2 cookies

DIFFICULTY:

Intermediate

INGREDIENTS

1¼ cups all-purpose flour

½ teaspoon baking powder

½ teaspoon baking soda

¼ teaspoon salt (kosher or sea)

¾ cup peanut butter, either chunky or creamy

6 tablespoons cannabutter, softened

⅓ cup packed brown sugar

⅓ cup granulated sugar

1 egg

1 teaspoon vanilla extract

¼ cup heavy cream

6 ounces bittersweet chocolate, chopped

½ cup crushed chocolate toffee (such as Heath)

PROCEDURE

1. Preheat the oven to 340° F. Line 3 baking sheets with parchment paper and set them aside.
2. In a medium bowl, combine the flour, baking powder, baking soda, and salt.
3. In the bowl of a stand mixer fitted with the paddle attachment (or use a hand mixer or a wooden spoon in a large bowl), combine the peanut butter, unsalted butter, cannabutter, brown sugar, and granulated sugar. Beat on medium speed until smooth.
4. Reduce the speed to low and add the egg and vanilla. Beat until well mixed, about 1 minute.
5. Add the flour mixture and mix until just combined.
6. Drop the dough by heaping tablespoons onto the prepared baking sheets, about 2 inches apart. Bake all 3 sheets at once until cookies are puffed and set, 7 to 9 minutes.
7. Make small indentations in each cookie with the handle of a wooden spoon.
8. Return the cookies to the oven, baking 5 to 6 minutes more or until golden brown.
9. While the cookies bake, combine the cream and chocolate in a double boiler or heat-proof pan set over just-simmering water, stirring to melt the chocolate.
10. Remove the cookies from the oven, and immediately spoon 1 teaspoon of the chocolate mixture into each indentation. Sprinkle toffee bits on top, mostly in the center. Transfer the cookies to a wire rack to cool completely.
11. Store cookies in an airtight container.

LEMON BARS

MAKES:

1 dozen bars

SERVING SIZE:

1 bar

DIFFICULTY:

Easy

Bright with lemon juice and zest, these tangy citrus bars have a slightly greenish hue when baked, due to the cannabutter in the filling.

INGREDIENTS

Cooking spray, for greasing the pan

For the crust:
1 cup all-purpose flour

¼ cup (½ stick) unsalted butter, softened

¼ cup cannabutter, softened

¼ cup confectioners' sugar

For the filling:
2 eggs

1 cup sugar

1 tablespoon freshly grated lemon zest (from 2 medium lemons)

2 tablespoons lemon juice (from 1 medium lemon)

½ teaspoon flour

¼ teaspoon salt (kosher or sea)

PROCEDURE

1. Preheat the oven to 340°F. Spray an 8- or 9-inch square pan with the cooking spray and set it aside.

Make the crust:

2. In a medium bowl, combine the flour, unsalted butter, cannabutter, and confectioners' sugar.
3. Using your fingers, press the crust evenly into the prepared pan.
4. Bake the crust until it is light golden brown, about 20 minutes. Transfer the pan to a wire rack to cool completely. Leave the oven on.

While the crust bakes, make the filling:

5. In a medium bowl, whisk together all the ingredients until fluffy.
6. Pour the filling over the cooled crust.
7. Bake until the filling is set, about 25 to 30 minutes.
8. Cool completely before cutting into bars.

TRICOLOR MARSHMALLOW CEREAL TREATS

MAKES:
9 treats

SERVING SIZE:
1 treat

DIFFICULTY:
Easy

Adding fruit flavors to the classic dessert of marshmallows and crisped-rice cereal gives it a whole new eye appeal. If you can't find freeze-dried fruit (usually found at upscale markets, health-food stores, or online), substitute ½ tablespoon each of three different jams of your choice.

INGREDIENTS

Baking spray

1.2 ounces freeze-dried strawberries

1.2 ounces freeze-dried blueberries

1.2 ounces freeze-dried mangoes

9 cups crisp rice cereal

½ cup (1 stick) plus 1 tablespoon unsalted butter

3 tablespoons cannabutter

5 ounces mini marshmallows

PROCEDURE

1. Coat a 9-inch square baking dish with baking spray and line with parchment paper, allowing 2 inches of overhang on each side.
2. In a completely dry blender, or in the bowl of a food processor fitted with the metal blade, pulse the strawberries until they become fruit dust.
3. Transfer the pulverized strawberries to a medium bowl, clean the blender or food processor, and repeat, separately, with the blueberries and mangoes, placing each fruit into its own bowl.
4. Add 3 cups of the cereal to each bowl. Toss to coat with the fruit dust.
5. In a small saucepan, melt the unsalted butter and cannabutter over medium-low heat. Gradually add the marshmallows, stirring until they are melted and combined.
6. Divide the marshmallow mixture among the three bowls, stirring well to combine.
7. Using your fingers, press the strawberry layer into the prepared baking dish.
8. Press the blueberry and mango layers into the dish over the strawberry layer.
9. Allow the treats to set at room temperature for a minimum of 30 minutes before removing from baking dish and cutting into bars.

CHEFS' NOTE

A fun variation is a peanut-butter-and-jelly version. Make two layers with ⅓ cup strawberry jam, and a layer with ¼ cup peanut butter in place of the freeze-dried berries, and sandwich the peanut butter layer in between the strawberry layers.

FIRECRACKERS

Firecrackers are a popular dessert among cannabis enthusiasts. They're like s'mores, but with chocolate-hazelnut spread and bananas in place of chocolate bars and marshmallows. Baked in the oven, these come out warm, gooey, and delicious.

MAKES:

2 firecrackers

SERVING SIZE:

1 firecracker

DIFFICULTY:

Easy

INGREDIENTS

¼ cup chocolate-hazelnut spread
(such as Nutella)

2 teaspoons canna-coconut oil

2 whole graham crackers,
broken in half

½ banana, sliced in rounds

PROCEDURE

1. Preheat the oven to 325°F.
2. In a small bowl, combine the chocolate-hazelnut spread with the canna-coconut oil.
3. Spread the hazelnut mixture equally on two cracker halves.
4. Top the spread with a few banana slices on each half. Put the other cracker halves on top to form a sandwich.
5. Wrap the firecrackers in aluminum foil and put them on a baking sheet.
6. Bake the firecrackers 10 to 12 minutes.
7. Open the packets carefully; they will be hot.

RASPBERRY-STUFFED CHOCOLATE CUPCAKES

These cupcakes are moist, luscious, and chocolaty, and the raspberry-jam center is a lovely surprise.

MAKES:

1 dozen cupcakes

SERVING SIZE:

1 cupcake

DIFFICULTY:

Easy

INGREDIENTS

Baking spray, for greasing

1 cup all-purpose flour

1 cup sugar

½ cup unsweetened cocoa powder

1 teaspoon instant espresso powder

1 teaspoon baking powder

½ teaspoon baking soda

½ teaspoon salt (kosher or sea)

½ cup milk

¼ cup cannaoil

1 egg

1 teaspoon vanilla extract

½ cup boiling water

¼ cup raspberry jam

¹⁄₃ cup semisweet chocolate chips

¼ cup heavy cream

12 raspberries

PROCEDURE

1. Preheat the oven to 340°F. Line a standard-size muffin pan with paper liners, spray the liners with cooking spray, and set the pan aside.
2. In a large bowl, whisk together the flour, sugar, cocoa and espresso powders, baking powder, baking soda, and salt.
3. In a medium bowl, whisk together the milk, cannaoil, egg, and vanilla.
4. Add the wet ingredients to the dry ingredients and combine well.
5. Add the boiling water and beat strenuously with a wooden spoon for 2 minutes.
6. Spoon the batter into the prepared liners, filling them halfway. Spoon 1 teaspoon raspberry jam in the center of each cupcake and top with more batter, filling the cups three-quarters full.
7. Bake until a toothpick inserted in the center of a cupcake comes out clean, 11 to 13 minutes.
8. Remove the pan to a wire rack to cool.
9. In a double boiler or heat-proof pan set over just-simmering water, combine the chocolate chips and cream, stirring to melt the chocolate. Spoon about 2 teaspoons of chocolate mixture onto the center of each cupcake and top with a sprinkling of cocoa powder and a fresh raspberry.

TRIPLE BOMB BROWNIES

Brownies and cannabis are such a cliché. But this recipe is fun to make, fun to eat, and it packs quite a punch. Starting with a commercial brownie mix speeds up the process considerably.

MAKES:
20–24 brownies

SERVING SIZE:
1 brownie

DIFFICULTY:
Easy

INGREDIENTS

Cooking spray, for greasing the pan

1 tablespoon instant espresso powder

2 teaspoons vanilla extract

2 boxes commercial brownie mix, prepared according to package directions (or batter for your favorite recipe for a 9-by-13-inch pan)

¼ cup Caramel Sauce (page 230)

⅓ cup Chocolate Sauce (page 233)

4 tablespoons almond paste

3 tablespoons cannabutter, softened

1 cup chocolate chips

PROCEDURE

1. Preheat the oven to 340°F. Coat a 9-by-13-inch pan with cooking spray and set it aside.
2. Add the espresso powder and vanilla to the prepared brownie batter.
3. Pour half of the batter into the pan.
4. Drizzle the caramel and chocolate sauces over the batter.
5. In a small bowl, combine the almond paste and cannabutter. Drop small pieces of the cannabutter mixture evenly over the batter.
6. Sprinkle the chocolate chips evenly over the batter.
7. Top with the remaining batter.
8. Bake until a toothpick inserted in the center of the brownies comes out clean, 35–40 minutes.
9. Remove the pan to a wire rack. Cool the brownies completely in the pan before cutting them into squares.

CHERRY COOKIE HAND PIES

These little hand pies have a cookie crust and a rich, sweet cherry center. Instead of cherry preserves, you can try lemon curd, chocolate-hazelnut spread, almond paste, or pretty much any other sweet filling your heart desires.

MAKES:

18 pies

SERVING SIZE:

1 pie

DIFFICULTY:

Intermediate/ Advanced

INGREDIENTS

2½ cups all-purpose flour, plus more for dusting the work surface

¼ teaspoon baking soda

¼ teaspoon salt (kosher or sea)

6 tablespoons (¾ stick) unsalted butter, softened

6 tablespoons cannabutter, softened

¾ cup granulated sugar

1 large egg

4 tablespoons milk, divided

1 teaspoon almond extract

½ cup cherry preserves

1 egg white

1 cup confectioners' sugar

½ teaspoon vanilla extract

PROCEDURE

1. Preheat the oven to 340°F. Line 2 baking sheets with parchment paper and set them aside.
2. In a medium bowl, whisk together the flour, baking soda, and salt.
3. In the bowl of a stand mixer fitted with the paddle attachment (or use a hand mixer or a wooden spoon in a large bowl), combine the unsalted butter, cannabutter, and granulated sugar. Beat on medium speed until fluffy.
4. Reduce the speed to low and add the egg, 2 tablespoons of the milk, and the almond extract. Beat until well mixed, about 1 minute.
5. Add the flour mixture in 3 batches, mixing between each addition. After adding the last of the flour mixture, scrape down the sides of the bowl and stir until just combined.
6. Lightly flour a work space. Divide the dough in half, and roll each half out to a ¼-inch thickness. Using a 2½-inch cookie cutter, cut out 36 rounds, gathering and rerolling the dough as necessary.
7. Put 18 of the rounds on the prepared sheets, spacing them 1 inch apart.
8. Place 1 heaping teaspoon of preserves in the center of each round. Top with the remaining rounds and crimp the sides together with a fork.
9. In a small bowl, lightly whisk the egg white and brush it on the tops of the pies. Cut a small X in the center of each pie top with a knife.
10. Bake the pies until the edges are slightly golden, about 12 minutes.
11. Remove the pies from the oven and let them cool completely on the baking sheets set on wire racks.
12. In a small bowl, whisk together the remaining 2 tablespoons milk, confectioners' sugar, and vanilla.
13. Brush the pies with the glaze and let sit for 30 minutes before eating.

GLUTEN-FREE ALMOND RASPBERRY CAKE

This cake has a fabulous moist texture. It's also gluten-free and freezes beautifully. For a special treat, we like to serve it warm (or warm it slightly in the oven) and add a dollop of ice cream.

MAKES:

1 9-inch cake

SERVES:

12

SERVING SIZE:

1 piece

DIFFICULTY:

Intermediate

INGREDIENTS

Cooking spray, for greasing the pan

½ cup (1 stick) unsalted butter, melted

¼ cup cannabutter, melted

1¼ cups plus 2 tablespoons sugar, divided

2 eggs, lightly beaten

1 tablespoon orange juice concentrate

2 teaspoons freshly grated orange zest

1 teaspoon almond extract

1½ cups of your favorite gluten-free flour (with a 1-to-1 ratio)

½ cup plus 2 tablespoons raspberry jam, divided

1 cup slivered or sliced almonds

¾ cup vanilla Greek yogurt, for garnish

PROCEDURE

1. Preheat the oven to 340°F. Spray a 9-inch cake pan with the cooking spray and set it aside.
2. In a large bowl, whisk together the unsalted butter, cannabutter, and 1¼ cups of the sugar.
3. Stir in the beaten eggs, mixing well. Stir in the orange juice concentrate, zest, and almond extract.
4. Stir in the flour until just mixed. Turn the batter into the prepared pan. Swirl ½ cup of the jam through the cake with a small spoon. Sprinkle the top of the cake with the almonds, followed by the remaining 2 tablespoons sugar.
5. Bake until the cake is golden and set or a toothpick inserted in the center comes out clean, 35 to 40 minutes.
6. Let the cake completely cool in the pan.
7. Just before serving, combine the yogurt in a small bowl with the remaining 2 tablespoons of jam and place a dollop on each slice.

CARROT CAKE

MAKES:

1 9-inch layer cake

SERVES:

12

SERVING SIZE:

1 piece

DIFFICULTY:

**Intermediate/
Advanced**

Carrot cake with cream cheese frosting always makes us think of autumn. In this recipe, the frosting, not the cake, contains cannabis. If you prefer your cake unfrosted, you can substitute ¼ cup (2 ounces) cannaoil for ¼ cup of the canola oil in the cake recipe. If you skip the frosting, we also recommend doubling the ginger in the cake to amplify the flavor.

INGREDIENTS

For the cake:
Cooking spray, for greasing the pan

2 cups all-purpose flour

1¾ teaspoons baking soda

2 teaspoons ground cinnamon

½ teaspoon ground nutmeg

½ teaspoon ground ginger

½ teaspoon salt (kosher or sea)

2⅔ cups grated carrots

1 cup chopped walnuts, ¼ cup reserved for decorating cake

1 cup canola oil

4 large eggs, lightly beaten

2 cups packed brown sugar

2 teaspoons vanilla extract

For the frosting:
1 pound cream cheese, softened

¼ cup cannabutter, softened

3 cups confectioners' sugar

1 tablespoon vanilla extract

Pinch of salt (kosher or sea)

PROCEDURE

Make the cake:

1. Preheat the oven to 340°F. Spray two 9-inch square cake pans with cooking spray and set them aside.
2. In a medium bowl, whisk together the flour, baking soda, cinnamon, nutmeg, ginger, and salt.
3. In the bowl of a stand mixer fitted with the paddle attachment (or use a hand mixer or a wooden spoon in a large bowl), combine the carrots, ¾ cup walnuts, oil, eggs, brown sugar, and vanilla on medium speed.
4. Reduce the speed to low, add the flour mixture, and mix until just blended, scraping down the bowl as needed.
5. Pour the batter into the prepared pans. Bake for 25 to 30 minutes, until a toothpick inserted in the center comes out with just a few crumbs on it.
6. Let the cakes cool in the pans.

While the cake cools, make the frosting:

7. In the bowl of a stand mixer fitted with the paddle attachment (or use a hand mixer or a wooden spoon in a large bowl), beat the cream cheese and cannabutter on medium speed until very smooth and creamy, 3 to 5 minutes.
8. Add the confectioners' sugar, vanilla, and salt and beat on medium-high until fluffy, about 3 minutes.
9. When the cakes have completely cooled, turn the first cake out onto a serving plate. Using an offset spatula, spread a little less than half the frosting over the top.
10. Turn out the second layer on top of the first and spread the remaining frosting over the top and sides of the cake. Sprinkle the reserved walnuts on top.

CARAMEL SAUCE

This caramel sauce is a dream topping for ice cream, amazing drizzled over waffles or pancakes, and a no-brainer for apple dipping.

MAKES:

1½ cups

SERVING SIZE:

¼ cup

DIFFICULTY:

Easy

INGREDIENTS

1 cup packed brown sugar

½ cup half-and-half

2 tablespoons unsalted butter

2 tablespoons cannabutter

Pinch of salt (kosher or sea)

2 teaspoons vanilla extract

PROCEDURE

1. In a medium saucepan, combine the brown sugar, half-and-half, butter, cannabutter, and salt over low heat, whisking constantly, until the sauce thickens enough to coat the back of a spoon, 5 to 7 minutes.
2. Remove the sauce from the heat and stir in the vanilla before serving.

CHOCOLATE SAUCE

We've never met a chocolate sauce we didn't like—and this recipe is no exception. Leftover sauce will keep in the fridge for one week. Note that all the sauces will harden as they cool; simply reheat the sauce over low heat to serve.

MAKES:

2 cups

SERVING SIZE:

¹⁄₃ cup

DIFFICULTY:

Easy

INGREDIENTS

1 cup heavy cream

2 tablespoons cannabutter

8 ounces dark chocolate, finely chopped

PROCEDURE

1. In a double boiler or heat-proof bowl set over just-simmering water, heat the cream and cannabutter, stirring occasionally to be sure the butter has melted.
2. When the butter has completely melted, add the chocolate. Stir until the chocolate has completely melted and the mixture is smooth.

STRAWBERRY SAUCE

Laurie freezes fresh, ripe berries all summer long so she can make this sauce the rest of the year. You can use fresh strawberries, but frozen berries from the grocery store work fine too. If you use frozen ones, you'll need to thaw them before proceeding with the recipe, and you may want to add a bit more honey. This sauce is great in smoothies, stirred into sparkling water or wine (such as prosecco), mixed into a vinaigrette, or used atop a dessert.

MAKES:

1½ cups

SERVING SIZE:

¼ cup

DIFFICULTY:

Easy

INGREDIENTS

1 pound strawberries, hulled and finely chopped

¼ cup honey

2 tablespoons canna-coconut oil

½ cup freshly squeezed orange juice (from 2 medium oranges)

2 teaspoons cornstarch

Pinch of salt (kosher or sea)

PROCEDURE

1. In a small saucepan, combine the strawberries, honey, and cannaoil and heat over medium-low heat.
2. In a small bowl, combine the orange juice with the cornstarch.
3. Add the cornstarch mixture to the berries and stir until the sauce begins to thicken and coats the back of a spoon, about 8-10 minutes. Remove from heat. (The sauce will continue to thicken as it cools.) Stir in the salt.

CHEFS' NOTE
For a triple-berry sauce, substitute fresh whole raspberries and blackberries
in place of some of the strawberries.

ENDNOTES

1. Evan-Mills.com. "Energy up in Smoke: The Carbon Footprint of Indoor *Cannabis* Production." Evan Mills. Accessed July 6, 2015. http://evan-mills.com/energy-associates/Indoor.html

2. Nlm.nih.gov. "Drug Abuse." US National Library of Medicine. Last modified February 8, 2013. Accessed July 6, 2015. http://www.nlm.nih.gov/medlineplus/ency/article/001945.htm.

3. Narconon.org. "History of Marijuana." Narconon International. Accessed July 6, 2015. http://www.narconon.org/drug-information/marijuana-history.html.

4. En.emetprize.org. "Emet Prize Laureates: Professor Rafael Mechoulam." The A.M.N. Foundation for the Advancement of Science, Art, and Culture. Accessed July 6, 2015. http://en.emetprize.org/laureates/exact-sciences/chemistry/prof-rafael-mechoulam.

5. Ncbi.nlm.nih.gov. "The Endocannabinoid System as an Emerging Target of Pharmacotherapy." Pál Pacher, Sándor Bátkai, George Kunos. http://www.ncbi.nlm.nih.gov/pubmed/?term=B%26%23x000c1%3BTKAIS%5Bauth%5DNational Center for Biotechnology Information; US National Library of Medicine. Accessed July 6, 2015. http://www.ncbi.nlm.nih.gov/pmc/articles/PMC2241751.

6. Ibid. "Terpenoids as Plant Antioxidants." Grassmann, J. National Center for Biotechnology Information; US National Library of Medicine. Accessed July 6, 2015. http://www.ncbi.nlm.nih.gov/pubmed/16492481.

7. Ibid. "Chemical Composition and Antibacterial, Antifungal and Antioxidant Activities of the Flower Oil of Retama raetam (Forssk.) Webb from Tunisia." Edziri, H.; Mastouri, M.; Cheraif, I.; Aouni, M. National Center for Biotechnology Information; US National Library of Medicine. Accessed July 6, 2015.

8. Ibid. "Taming THC: potential cannabis synergy and phytocannabinoid-terpenoid entourage effects." Ethan B. Russo. National Center for Biotechnology Information; US National Library of Medicine; *British Journal of Pharmacology*. http://www.ncbi.nlm.nih.gov/pmc/articles/PMC3165946.

9. Cnn.com. "Marijuana Stops Child's Severe Seizures." Saundra Young. CNN. Last modified August 7, 2013. Accessed July 6, 2015. http://www.cnn.com/2013/08/07/health/charlotte-child-medical-marijuana.

10. Peter B. Kaufman, *Natural Products from Plants* (Boca Raton, Florida: CRC Press LLC, 1999).

11. Raco.cat. "Sistemes I Processos: Terpenoids and Plant Communication." Joan Llusià, Marc Estiarte, Josep Peñuelas. Accessed July 6, 2015. http://www.raco.cat/index.php/ButlletiICHN/article/viewFile/175225/227576.

12. Sclabs.com. "Terpenes." SC Labs. Last modified September 12, 2014. Accessed July 6, 2015. http://sclabs.com/learn/terpenes.html.

13. Dr. Duke's Phytochemical and Ethnobotanical Databases. "Chemicals in: *Hyptis suaveoloens* POIT." James A. Duke, Mary Jo Bogenschutz. Accessed July 6, 2015. http://www.ars-grin.gov/cgi-bin/duke/farmacy2.pl?494.

14. Chem.uwec.edu. "Flavanoids as Antioxidants." Peir-Giorgio Pietta. Last modified September 13, 1999. Accessed July 6, 2015. http://www.chem.uwec.edu/Chem491_W01/Pharmacognosy%20491/flavonoid.pdf.

15. Edenbotanicals.com. "Extraction Methods." Eden Botanicals. Accessed July 6, 2015. http://www.edenbotanicals.com/extraction-methods.

16. Drugandalcoholdependence.com. "Exercise Increases Plasma THC Concentrations in Regular Cannabis Users." Jonathan C. Arnold, Jessica Booth, Raimondo Bruno, et al. Drug and Alcohol Dependence. Accessed July 6, 2015. http://www.drugandalcoholdependence.com/article/S0376-8716(13)00296-2/abstract.

ABOUT THE CHEFS

Laurie Wolf is a writer and recipe developer. She graduated from the Culinary Institute of America and has worked as a chef, caterer, and food stylist and is the owner of Laurie & MaryJane, purveyor of award-winning marijuana-infused foods. She is a regular contributor to the _Denver Post_'s new marijuana section, the Cannabist, and writes for magazines such as _High Times_, _Oregon Leaf_, and _Cannabis Now_. Her previous works include _Food Lovers' Guide to Portland, Oregon_ and _Portland, Oregon Chef's Table_.

Melissa Parks is a classically trained chef. She attended Le Cordon Bleu and Johnson & Wales University and obtained degrees in culinary arts, baking and pastry, and culinary nutrition. Her previous experience includes research and development for General Mills, serving as a private chef and wedding-cake designer, and comanaging multiple Colorado-area bakeries. She now dedicates herself to creating medicated edibles that provide the rewarding THC experience while still tasting delicious.

ABOUT HERB

HERB is the world's number-one resource for cannabis recipes, information, and culture. Formerly The Stoner's Cookbook, the company was founded in 2006 by Dan Crothers and Lucas Young to revolutionize the industry, with the ultimate goal of enabling people to legally, safely, and enjoyably consume cannabis. Its mission is to elevate the conversation around cannabis and fuel change to help end the social harms caused by prohibition. Now, newly rebranded as HERB, this small team of dedicated individuals continues to provide the premier source for recipes and information about cooking with cannabis. Their website, Herb.co, is the most active community in the cannabis industry and reaches over 25 million people a week.

ABOUT THE PHOTOGRAPHER

Bruce Wolf is an award-winning photographer whose career has included ad campaigns for Nikon, Jenn-Air, Viking, G.E., Home Depot, and Harley-Davidson, among others. Bruce has worked for magazines including *Vogue*, *Martha Stewart Living*, *House Beautiful*, *H.G.*, *Metropolitan Home*, and more. However, nothing is as rewarding as working with his wife, Laurie Wolf.

ACKNOWLEDGMENTS

It must be the case for any writer that assembling thoughts into a single book is a journey, sometimes difficult but always enlightening. Along this journey I made new friends, traveled to a new city, and created art with incredibly talented individuals who share not only a passion for the cannabis movement but also a love of food. The recipes are a unique intersection of culinary arts, chemistry, and cannabis, resulting in what for me is a labor of love. The experience will remain with me always.

To start I have to thank the team at HERB. They started this project, and really saw it through to the end. The countless hours of organizing, phone calls, and working clear into the wee hours of the night did not go unnoticed or unappreciated. I wish you all continued success in all you do!

There are many people who have assisted me through this process, and one in particular has become a friend for life, Laurie Wolf. Laurie, thank you! Thank you for your ability to communicate with love and compassion, thank you for being my fellow culinary "partner in crime," and thank you for making me laugh when I needed it the most. You are a gem, and I couldn't have asked for a better partner for this project.

I also have to thank the extremely talented and gifted photographer Bruce Wolf. His ability to bring our food to life, on a page, was no easy task. Yet his expertise made it all appear effortless. Thank you for your time, effort, and patience.

I couldn't write this without acknowledging the support of both my parents: Susan and Patrick Parks, with a particular appreciation for the technical help provided by my father.

Very early on I was introduced to an author whose works I have read and admired for years: Michael Ruhlman. He is not only a celebrated author, chef, and entrepreneur; he is also one of the most humble individuals I have ever met. His generosity with his time and energy blew me away. Michael shared his experiences as an author and advice on how to tackle projects such as *Herb*, and he ultimately became quite the mentor for a novice author. His assistance has proven to be invaluable. Thank you, Michael.

Lastly I would like to thank the industry that has welcomed me with open arms, that encourages me to try harder, and that pushes me every day to learn and grow and ultimately pay it forward. Cannabis aids many people, in countless ways, but for me the plant has helped me find my place in life as a chef.

—**Melissa Parks**

I would like to thank the HERB guys for being an absolute pleasure to work with. Dan, Matt, and Lucas were smart, fun, open, and delightful. Lucas and I laughed through all our conversations—that is, when I finally understood his charming Kiwi accent! One of the joys of this kind of crazy business is the mostly fabulous people you meet. (Just about everyone I meet is a grower, and some are the last people I would suspect.)

Working with canna-chef Melissa Parks was a treat. Our relationship began online and has blossomed into a terrific friendship, with shared interests and sensibilities. Melissa is a font of canna-knowledge, not to mention easygoing and lots of fun.

To "the Mary," Mary Thigpen, for her ability to make hard things easy and easy things enjoyable. She is smart and capable. The better I get to know her, the more I love her. These days I spend much time with her, and we always have fun. She will soon be a Wolf.

To my husband and photographer, Bruce Wolf: I know of no one who takes a better photograph. He is the only guy I know who can actually make chicken salad out of chicken shit! The light that he creates when he works borders on magical. We have been working and living together for more than thirty-five years. How crazy is that? We laugh a lot and he takes gorgeous pictures. Thanks, Bruce.

To my adult kids, Nick and Olivia: Thanks for being behind your mom's crazy new business and turning out so great after growing up in our strange, pet-filled home. (I have no idea how I would have turned out if I had been raised by me.) We are the "Wolf Cartel." I love you both so, so much, and am very proud of you.

And to Matt, Fred, and Geri . . . always.

Thanks to our Oregon friends, who have welcomed us with warmth, humor, and a love of the great outdoors. (Some might call it a peculiar obsession.) "It is nice out there," she says, looking out the window.

To Dr. F. and Ruth C. for helping me get my head on straight.

Shout-out to Zim, T., Kip, Oscar, Megan, Kara, Sam, Jeff, Kat, Michael, and Ramin. Love to Steve F., Kate, and nature Dave. To the peanut-butter people—love you guys.

To Alex, at Chem History, for making all our testing a delightful experience.

To David M. and his lovely bride, Freddi: The fact that you believe in us makes me happier than I could ever say. The generosity of your time and earning your confidence are things I won't forget. There are no words, except for these.

To the folks I have met in this new canna-venture, from the growers to the dispensary folks to the people on the committees who are working to get this plant the full appreciation it deserves, thank you for sharing this adventure. I have been enjoying weed on and off for forty-five years. It's my favorite herb.

To all my Roost buds: Megan, Mia, Caleb, Leo, Ciaran (Butler), Jordan, and sometimes Stephanie. Love you all.

To Lisa and Rob for being amazing. Feeding us terrific food, making us laugh, and hoping that their positive energy is catching. (I hear it rubs off, but you have to really scrub.)

To skinny, delightful, and charming—you know who you are. Or do you? Well, you should—we love you all.

To the Micks, who are friends with us despite what I do for a living!

Thanks, everyone. What a short, strange trip it's been.

—Laurie Wolf

The team at HERB—Lucas, Matt, and Daniel—would like to express our deep and heartfelt thanks and gratitude to everyone who worked tirelessly to bring this book to fruition. Tight budgets and short deadlines brought out the best in everyone, and we couldn't be happier with the result or prouder of our team.

We'd like to thank:

- Our chefs, Melissa Parks and Laurie Wolf, who managed to deliver so many expertly crafted recipes that we are sure you're going to enjoy;
- Bruce Wolf, whose photography amazed us all and brought out the textures and colors of the chefs' work in the most mouthwatering way;
- The team at Inkshares, who helped us raise the money to bring this book to life and managed the very complex processes involved;
- Girl Friday Productions, who worked with almost impossible deadlines to bring this book to you on time;
- And, of course, we'd especially like to thank our backers. Three thousand people pre-ordered this book and supported its production. A special shout-out to two of the biggest backers, Theron Graham Landes and Alexander Andrawes. Thanks, guys!

—Lucas Young, cofounder and CTO at HERB

INDEX

INKSHARES

Inkshares is a crowdfunded book publisher. We democratize publishing by having readers select the books we publish—we edit, design, print, distribute, and market any book that meets a pre-order threshold.

Interested in making a book idea come to life? Visit inkshares.com to find new book projects or to start your own.